# Labour-management cooperation in SMEs: Forms and factors

# Labour-management cooperation in SMEs

## Forms and factors

Tayo Fashoyin
Emily Sims
Arturo Tolentino

INTERNATIONAL LABOUR OFFICE • GENEVA

Fashoyin, T.; Sims, E.; Tolentino, A.
*Labour–management cooperation in SMEs: Forms and factors*
Geneva, International Labour Office, 2006

ISBN 978-92-2-117413-4

ILO descriptors: labour relations, human resources management, small enterprise, small scale industry, food processing, Botswana, Kenya, Nepal, Philippines.
13.06.1

*ILO Cataloguing in Publication Data*

Typeset by Magheross Graphics, France & Ireland *www.magheross.com*
Printed in Switzerland

# PREFACE

This study offers an in-depth look at the ways in which small and medium-sized companies develop partnerships between managers and workers to increase productivity and competitiveness. The existing literature on labour–management cooperation in SMEs is thin, and this study makes an important contribution to the field. Key areas examined include:

- why labour–management cooperation is important for SMEs;

- the key prerequisites for developing effective cooperation concerning respect for workers' rights, conditions of work, and human resources management systems;

- the motivating factors – environmental, market, and idiosyncratic – for developing cooperation in SMEs;

- existing obstacles to cooperation; and

- the concrete benefits of cooperation realized by the particular enterprises studied.

The study is unique in several respects. It provides a comprehensive look at cooperation, examining a range of factors that may influence the degree to which firms give priority to cultivating cooperation, and the form that cooperation takes. The study concentrates on the food-processing sector, which allows for more detailed analysis, including backward and forward linkages, which are particularly significant for most developing countries. It also focuses exclusively on developing countries, adding an important dimension missing from most academic studies. Lastly, the detailed case studies, which include interviews from both managers and workers from a range of enterprises, contribute substantially to advancing beyond stereotypes to a better understanding of the reality entrepreneurs and workers face in SMEs.

v

This study will be of use to those who are interested in improving productivity and job quality. This includes national productivity centres, policy-makers, human resources advisors, business development services providers, business school professors and consultants. Entrepreneurs and managers may also find it useful to learn from other firms' experiences. Furthermore, trade unions can benefit from understanding better many of the factors influencing the strategic choices firms make in developing cooperative strategies with workers, in particular with trade unions.

This study is a collaborative effort between the ILO's Social Dialogue, Labour Law and Labour Administration Department and the Job Creation and Enterprise Development Department, and draws on the technical expertise of each department. We would like to thank Tayo Fashoyin, Emily Sims and Arturo Tolentino for their contributions.

*Johanna Walgrave*
*Director*
*Social Dialogue, Labour Law and*
*Labour Administration Department*
*International Labour Office*

*Michael Henriques*
*Director*
*Job Creation and*
*Enterprise Development Department*
*International Labour Office*

Geneva, 2006

# CONTENTS

# Figures

# Boxes

# ACKNOWLEDGEMENTS

The authors would like to thank the case contributors: N.C. Chune, Professor Kunle Iyanda S.M. Machuka, Dr Narayanb Manandhar, Ms Mary Leian C. Marasigan, J.O.Omolo, J.N. Onkunya, Professor Juan S.FA.. Palafox, Ms Melisa R. Serrano and Ms Catalina M. Tolentino.

We thank Johanna Walgrave, Director of the Social Dialogue, Labour Law and Labour Administration DepartmentIFP/Dialogue and Michael Henriques, Director of the Job Creation and Enterprise Development Department EMP/ENT for their support for the project.

Lastly, we thank Karin Fenczak for her research assistance, Irina Akimova for her assistance in layouts, Sandeep Prasad for his editorial assistance, and the anonymous reviewers for their comments.

# INTRODUCTION

# 1

Productive and competitive enterprises are essential for decent work, that is, employment which ensures a minimum standard for the safety, security and well-being of workers, and respect for their rights. Enterprises which are able to survive, expand and grow are able to create and sustain jobs. Decent work, in turn, is a prerequisite for enterprises to sustain and continuously improve their productivity and competitiveness in order to remain viable. Enterprises which place a high priority on the safety and well-being of workers, respect their rights, and engage them fully in the production process are much better positioned to take on the challenges of global markets, increasing competition, and ever more demanding customers.

In short, there is a symbiotic relationship between the economic and social performance of an enterprise. This is true for enterprises of any size. The main objective of this study is to better understand how labour–management partnership for productivity and competitiveness has developed in some small and medium-sized enterprises (SMEs) in selected developing countries; and to better understand the factors which can, on the one hand, impede the formation of labour–management cooperation, and those on the other which can foster cooperation and contribute to the creation of decent work in productive and competitive enterprises.

## Characteristics of SMEs influencing labour–management cooperation

Small and medium-sized enterprises can be found in all sectors, including extraction, manufacturing, construction, wholesale trade, retail trade, transportation and communications, producer services and personal services. SMEs are defined in various ways, and the definition varies greatly according to national conditions. The definition adopted by a particular country is usually based on the size and structure of the sectors concerned and on the use and objectives for which the definition is formulated (regulation, administration, policy development, and so on). The Organisation for Economic Co-operation and Development (OECD) defines establishments with up to 19 employees as "very small"; from 20 to 99 as "small"; from 100 to 499 as "medium"; and with over 500 as "large". However, in many developing countries a "medium-sized" firm is in fact relatively large. And firms with highly seasonal demand are difficult to classify; for instance, a firm such as a food-processing plant with few permanent employees may triple its number of employees during harvest season.

Other definitions of SMEs include the amount of capital invested, total assets, the volume of output or sales, production capacity, or the use of energy. The independence of the small enterprise is also a criterion, i.e. not being a subsidiary or production unit of a larger firm. In the European Union, for example, an enterprise cannot have 25 per cent or more of its control in the hands of a larger enterprise and still be considered a small enterprise. These definitions also have limitations. For instance, a firm may have a high level of assets or use highly sophisticated technology, and yet have a very simple management structure (ILO, 1997).

One characteristic, however, that clearly sets SMEs apart from larger firms is the management structure and system of the enterprise. SMEs are closely linked with the practice of entrepreneurship, where the strategic and operational management decision-making primarily rests with one or two persons who typically own the enterprise.

Typically, the entrepreneur has a very close and intimate identification with his or her small business which strongly influences the forms of labour–management cooperation which evolve over the life-cycle of the enterprise. The strong influence of the personality of the entrepreneur can limit the development of labour–management cooperation, particularly in the early stages of development of the enterprise. However, market forces are now having the opposite effect, predisposing entrepreneur–managers to search for ways to foster greater labour–management cooperation. Awareness is growing among entrepreneur–managers that labour–management partnership is essential for SMEs to compete in global markets.

SMEs are a major source of existing employment and job growth. However, they are also vulnerable to volatile markets and have low survival rates. They generally lag behind larger enterprises concerning income for workers and the owner, conditions of work, job security, health and safety, opportunities for training and representation. The way in which they organize and manage productivity improvement affects their profitability, competitiveness, social performance and contribution to the economy and society, and ultimately their survival. Understanding how labour–management partnership develops in SMEs and the forces encouraging or deterring that development is an important first step in helping such enterprises to become more productive and competitive.

## The link between productivity, competitiveness and promotion of decent work in SMEs

Productivity is a major concern of all enterprises, but is particularly important for the survival and expansion of SMEs. It is a fundamental measure of company performance and profitability, and a key indicator of a firm's prospects for survival. Productivity refers to the relationship between the output generated and the input needed to create that output. But the concept has been refined over time. Productivity used to be seen mainly as an efficiency goal to maximize the ratio of output to input. Now the notion of productivity increasingly emphasizes both efficiency and effectiveness – how efficiently an enterprise uses its resources (labour, capital, land, materials, energy and information) to meet more effectively the changing needs and expectations of customers (utility, quality, uniqueness, convenience, availability, and so on). Even the notion of outputs and inputs is changing: outputs and inputs are increasingly recognized as including the social and ecological impacts of the production–distribution processes.

Higher productivity assures a company's competitiveness and growth. Competitiveness refers to the ability to produce goods and services that can compete in local and international markets while maintaining a high standard of living for people. In a very dynamic market environment, an enterprise's competitiveness is not based on cost and price alone but increasingly on customer orientation, speed, flexibility, agility and the ability to innovate and to provide value for money, as well as social performance.

Productivity and competitiveness are of concern to workers, for productivity growth makes possible the growth of wages and benefits for those in employment, and the growth of jobs for those seeking work. Furthermore, productivity improvement has a fundamental impact on the economy, and hence improves the well-being of society as a whole.

## Labour–management partnership: The source of symbiosis between decent work and enterprise productivity and competitiveness

Labour–management partnership is the key to creating a virtuous circle between productivity and decent work in an enterprise. Labour–management partnership means that the entrepreneur–manager and workers see themselves and each other as key stakeholders in the business and join efforts to achieve enterprise productivity and profitability for their mutual benefit and the benefit of other stakeholders.

Partnership involves shared goals, efforts, and information. It also facilitates learning – workers and managers are more open and receptive to learning new ways of doing things and to learning from each other when they view themselves as a team, value each member of the team, and ensure that everyone on the team benefits from making an effort. In this sharing and learning environment innovativeness, flexibility and rapid response to market shifts become easier to achieve.

Labour–management partnership is essential to improve productivity and competitiveness.

It has long been recognized that there are positive linkages between harmonious labour–management relations and productivity improvement (Rosow and Casner-Lotto, 1994). Owing to increasing globalization, widespread trade liberalization, the internationalization of consumer preferences and the rapid advance of information and production technology, it is more necessary than ever for the partners to consult each other and collaborate on issues of vital importance to the survival and growth of the enterprise. There is therefore an intensified interest in developing new forms of labour–management relationships and new organizational structures and processes based on consultation, collaboration and participation, that will help enterprises cope with an increasingly competitive business environment.

ILO recognition of the need for labour–management cooperation is not entirely new. As far back as 1944, the General Conference of the International Labour Organization reiterated the mandate of the ILO to promote, inter alia, cooperation between labour and management in the continuous improvement of productive efficiency (the Declaration of Philadelphia). This idea is further spelled out in the Cooperation at the Level of the Undertaking Recommendation (No. 94) adopted by the International Labour Conference in 1952. The Recommendation calls for the promotion of consultation within the enterprise on matters of mutual concern not dealt with in collective bargaining or other machinery concerned with the determination of terms and conditions of employment. Furthermore, the Recommendation encourages instituting such consultation through voluntary agreements between parties. It also provides that consultation and cooperation may be promoted, as an alternative to or in combination with voluntary agreement, by laws or regulations establishing appropriate bodies for this purpose as well as their scope, function and structure. The Recommendation is very brief, and merely lays down the general principles without specifying details as to particular subjects for, or specific forms of, consultation and cooperation. Countries and enterprises are to develop the specific mechanisms according to their particular situation and need, national custom and practice, and industrial relations situation.

In this era of the globalization of markets, competitiveness is a phenomenon of considerable interest to most organizations, and one in which fundamental policy redirection continues to gain favour. The social partners share the general view that an improved standard of living depends on the capability of organizations to achieve high levels of productivity and to increase productivity over time.

In their book *The mutual gains enterprise*, T. Kochan and P. Osterman (1994) strongly support the view that competitive advantage in liberalized markets is achieved and sustained through the people working in the enterprise. They identify those elements of labour–management partnership and cooperation which are fundamental to the mutual gains enterprise, that is, the enterprise which promotes decent work while remaining productive and competitive (box 1).

---

Box 1    Principles guiding the mutual gains enterprise

**Strategic level**

- Supportive business strategies

- Top management commitment

- Effective voice for human resources in strategy making and governance

**Functional (human resource policy) level**

- Staffing based on employment stabilization

- Investment in training and development

- Contingent compensation that reinforces cooperation, participation, and contribution

**Workplace level**

- High standard of employee selection

- Broad task design and teamwork

- Employee involvement in problem solving

- Climate of cooperation and trust

Source: Kochan and Osterman, 1994.

---

This book explores how the small enterprises studied have applied these principles in their daily operations.

There is a synergistic relationship between strengthening labour–management partnership and strengthening other forms of social dialogue involving representation and voice, as well as dialogue concerning other workplace issues such as health and safety, and equality. Thus, strengthening labour–management partnership is a pragmatic way of promoting decent work, and decent work is a means of fostering labour–management partnership.

## Earlier studies

Early conventional wisdom romanticized labour–management relations in SMEs (see for example Schumacher, 1974). In such firms, workers' easy access to the most senior levels of management and the familial social relations were thought to create an environment which facilitates the resolution of grievances, or a communication mechanism that enables workers to freely relate to managers on a host of employment and work-related issues. Researchers found that in smaller firms there was less conflict; and generally concluded that this was due to greater day-to-day interaction between workers and the highest levels of managers. Such close proximity was held to strengthen relations between workers and the employer, and to promote a spirit of cooperation, mutual respect and moral attachment. Therefore, the argument went, workers in SMEs sought employment there because they valued such a collegial environment, and had a different attitude to work which explained the lower level of industrial action and lower rates of trade unionism than in larger firms; and there was little need for workers' organizations for collective action.

This paradigm started to be challenged in the late 1970s and 1980s by researchers cautioning against exaggerating the closeness of labour–management relations in small firms. They argued that workers in SMEs tended to be there simply because there were limited options elsewhere, owing to lack of skills, a slack labour market, or inability to relocate to other options. Furthermore, researchers such as Goss (1991) showed that industrial harmony was not a consequence of individual employee attitudes since there is little difference in attitude between workers in small and large enterprises; the only difference was in industrial action and rates of unionization. Other researchers have argued that the romantic view of smaller firms obscures their exploitative tendencies (Currant et al., 1993; Wilkinson, 1999; Wray, 1996; Rannie, 1999), or described small firms as "black hole" organizations. (Dundon, 1999; Guest and Conway, 1997). This alternative view paints a negative picture of small firms where authoritarian control reigns, resulting in poor working conditions and an unsafe working environment. Researchers have noted that such workplaces are typically non-union and asserted that managers and workers delude themselves into believing in the existence of a conflict-free work environment (Sisson, 1993; Edwards, 1995).

Today the view of quality of work in SMEs is still divided into two camps. Some studies show that workers in SMEs generally feel it is a more satisfying and humanizing work environment. For instance, a study conducted by the ILO found that workers in selected SMEs in Japan preferred working in a smaller and less institutional environment (ILO, 1997). (See more generally Bolton in Dundon et al, 1999; Roberts et al, 1992.) However, it is also widely recognized that wages and benefits tend to be lower in SMEs than in larger enterprises, even though there is substantial variation between SMEs, which often has more to do with whether they operate in the formal economy than with size per se (Sengenberger et al, 1990).

To a large extent, the characterization of SMEs as either "good" or "bad" enterprises is an over-simplification of the otherwise complex and dynamic market, and operational and public policy environment, in which smaller firms operate. Small firms have their own unique characteristics, which are often dictated by changing circumstances in a dynamic evolutionary process. As Kinnie et al. (1999) stress, external pressures such as changing market conditions have a significant effect on the nature of the fluid employment relationship in small firms.

An objective of this study is to look more closely at how well characterizations of labour–management cooperation pertain to small enterprises in four developing countries.

## About the case studies

The case study method is widely recognized as an important complement to quantitative research (Yin, 1984). Case studies allow for a detailed contextual analysis of a limited number of enterprises, to more clearly identify relationships between conditions and management decision-making; this helps the researcher to capture more completely the surrounding cultural, legal, economic and market context in which the enterprise operates. This is particularly important in researching enterprise culture since it is influenced by a wide range of variables. The in-depth interview approach used in the case study method also allows the researcher to hear the voices of those interviewed in more detail,[1] and gives a richer understanding of why people choose to cooperate or not.

---

[1] This study is stronger in capturing the voices of managers than of workers, although workers were also interviewed. This is probably due to the study's focus on a broad combination of internal and external factors influencing labour–management partnership (market structure, technologies, debt structure, and so on), the limited experience of the researchers in interviewing workers on their perspectives concerning management decision-making, and a reluctance of workers to speak more freely with researchers. The ILO is currently undertaking a parallel study which engages trade unionists as researchers to prepare case studies on labour–management cooperation.

The study design was based on the general methodology for case study (see for example Eisenhardt, 1989) and included five steps:

1. Identifying conflicting theories in the literature on labour–management cooperation in SMEs.

2. Identifying researchers in the field with extensive knowledge of the local context and subject matter.

3. Guiding researchers in developing questionnaires and interview structures, to ensure possibilities for using additional interviews and documentation to confirm the accuracy of what has been conveyed in an interview. The research included: background research on the economy, laws, industry structure, market structure, and history of the particular firm; quantitative research on company market and financial performance and records on collective agreements, conditions of work, grievances, strikes, number of worker suggestions, and other indications of industrial relations and labour–management cooperation; and qualitative interviews with top managers, line managers and workers in individual and group interviews. A tripartite validation workshop was held in the Philippines to test the accuracy of those findings.

4. Analysing cases. The cases were analysed at three levels: analysis of each firm's labour–management cooperation structure in comparison with its unique characteristics influencing cooperative strategies; analysis of groups of firms within the same country, to identify shared local factors; and across firms, to identify those factors which go beyond local contexts.

5. Writing up the manuscript. The draft manuscript was circulated back to case writers to check for accuracy of descriptions and plausibility of analysis and interpretation.

The cases were selected in consultation with local employers' organizations in each country, which drew up initial lists of recommended companies. The initial lists were then reduced, based primarily on managers' and workers' willingness to be interviewed in depth. However, other considerations – such as gender diversity, security, obtaining a range of management approaches and not only "good practices" – were also taken into account in order to have a more complete picture of the reality in SMEs. Of course, there is always some self-selection, and therefore bias, in the case study method, as not all enterprises are willing or able to spend an extended period of time with a research team. However, this study does not seek to draw universal conclusions based on a large random sample, but rather to flesh out existing knowledge of factors influencing cooperation in some, although not necessarily all, enterprises.

Criteria used to make the final selection included: willingness to participate, size, years in business, presence of some form of labour–management cooperation, location, i.e., a purposive method for selecting case companies was used. The 12 enterprises selected demonstrate a range of efforts to develop labour–management cooperation: some have made substantial progress while others still have quite a way to go. All the enterprises are registered and operate in the formal economy.

The enterprises are located in four countries: Botswana, Kenya, Nepal and the Philippines.[2] The study focuses on enterprises in developing countries because, although researchers in industrialized countries are beginning to pay more attention to labour–management cooperation in SMEs, few such case studies exist for enterprises in developing countries.

The enterprises are all located in the food-processing sector. This sector was chosen because of its strong backward linkage to the rural economy and hence to rural poverty alleviation. The food-processing sector also has a substantial percentage of women entrepreneurs and workers. And it is relatively diverse in terms of products and production processes, ranging from labour-intensive to capital-intensive activities. The food-processing sector was also chosen for this study as a follow-up to the ILO Tripartite Meeting on Technology and Employment in the Food and Drink Industries (see ILO, 1998). The conclusions of that meeting noted that: in developing countries, 90–95 per cent of food-processing enterprises are SMEs; in many developing countries, the food-processing industry is the largest employer and producer of value-added goods and is a major stimulus for growth owing to its backward and forward linkages; and the average share of the cost of raw materials to total operating costs ranges between 50 and 80 per cent while that of labour costs ranges from 5 to 20 per cent, so there is ample room to improve the productivity of non-labour inputs through labour–management cooperation as a viable strategy to improve the performance of the enterprise.

Enterprises with between 20 and 280 regular employees were selected, with most having less than 100, as there are still very few studies and materials on labour–management relations and practices in this enterprise size. In four of the twelve cases, workers were formally organized and affiliated with a trade union organization. In one additional case, the workers had been organized but had voted to dissolve the trade union.

---

[2] This study is the first in a series of planned studies which will cover several sectors and regions of the world. Due to budget constraints, Latin American and Caribbean countries could not be covered in this first phase.

Although the enterprises are all genuine, their names have been changed as part of an agreement to encourage those interviewed to be as candid as possible. The Annex provides a short description of each enterprise.

## General findings of the study

The firms reviewed in this study all demonstrated an awareness of the need for partnership. However, the strength of the partnership varied substantially between enterprises.

The cases indicate that each firm determines how much to invest in developing labour-management cooperation based on a complex and unique set of internal and external factors, depicted in figure 3 on page 95. No one factor dominates in determining whether partnership exists and which forms it takes. Environmental factors (legislation, structure of the sector, intensity of competition, and so on) and factors which are idiosyncratic to the entrepreneur both have an influence. However, the only factor with any significant predictive value about a firm's decision to invest in cooperation is its business strategy. Although the business strategy is substantially shaped by the other factors, it is not determined by them (which explains the relatively weak predictive value of the other factors). Rather, business strategy is a choice which management largely controls. Furthermore, the cases show that for many small firms, a low level of cooperation is due less to unwillingness of management to invest than to limited capacity. Hence, policy makers who are interested in raising the productivity of small enterprises in a country should focus more on helping them to build their capacity to develop labour–management cooperation.

Concerning conditions of work and rights of workers, a key element determining the potential for cooperation is the willingness of management to respect and take seriously the rights of workers, in particular the right to organize (irrespective of whether the workers actually choose to organize), or whether management wastes a lot of energy undermining workers' efforts to organize. Likewise, workers' willingness (individually or through their representative organizations) to participate in work teams, labour–management councils and similar forums plays a key role in enabling an enterprise to build cooperation.

Most importantly, the cases clearly demonstrate that the state of labour–management cooperation in an enterprise is not static. It changes over time as the mix of influential factors changes. Consequently, it is possible to develop partnership even in firms with very low levels of cooperation at present, *if* management and workers are willing to make the necessary investment. Likewise, firms with strong partnerships must continue to invest in the relationship, to ensure that both sides appreciate each other and continue to value working together.

## Structure of the book

Chapter 2 describes the growing importance of labour–management cooperation in light of increasing globalization and the changing nature of productivity, and explains the importance of labour–management cooperation in helping firms to adjust to these changes.

Chapter 3 analyses the specific forms labour–management cooperation takes in the firms studied.

Chapter 4 examines the specific forms of labour relations practices that exist. Topics covered include policy and practices concerning: staffing, recruitment, wages and compensation, performance appraisal and reward systems, and discipline and grievance procedures. It also looks closely at the impact on building labour–management cooperation of respect for the right to organize.

Chapter 5 examines specific factors which influence the form and extent of labour–management cooperation in particular firms. Issues examined include: market structures, regulations affecting SMEs and how they are enforced, characteristics of the entrepreneur, debt structure, proximity of workers and managers, and relations with suppliers, customers and the community.

Chapter 6 provides concluding observations.

• The Annex provides a short description of each enterprise, together with a table showing specific information.

# THE GROWING IMPORTANCE OF LABOUR–MANAGEMENT COOPERATION

# 2

Small and medium-sized enterprises face increasing competition as markets continue to globalize. World merchandise exports rose over a one-year period from 2002 to 2003 by 16 per cent to US$ 7.3 trillion and commercial services exports by 12 per cent to US$ 1.8 trillion; by 2004 the value of world merchandise trade had risen an additional 21 per cent to US$ 8.88 trillion, and that of world commercial services trade by an additional 16 per cent to US$2.10 trillion (World Trade Organization (WTO), 2004 and 2005). Trade between industrialized and developing economies is now increasingly in competing products, as opposed to the previous trend of developing countries exporting mostly raw materials and developed countries exporting mostly finished products (Ghose, 2003).

This rapid move towards greater integration of markets around the world is fuelled by a number of distinct yet interdependent forces:

- the spreading political decisions of countries to move towards trade liberalization and adoption of market-oriented economies. This is supported and encouraged by new institutions and agreements, such as the WTO and regional free trade agreements such as North American Free Trade Agreement (NAFTA), Asian Free Trade Area (AFTA);

- the freer flow of capital, both foreign direct investments and portfolio investments; and

- the spread and advance of global telecommunications, increased access to knowledge and information and vast improvements in transport systems; these changes are leading to the internationalization of customer preferences and expectations, resulting in very discriminating customers who are demanding more product differentiation and specialization. The fads and fashions not only spread rapidly across the globe but also shift and change very quickly. The rapid advances in information and

13

production technology make product obsolescence very fast. Product variety is thus increasing but the product life cycle is decreasing.

These forces have a direct impact on SMEs regardless of whether they produce for international or domestic markets.

## The changing nature of productivity

Globalization is changing the notion of productivity. Productivity is a measure of how efficiently and effectively an enterprise uses its resources – labour, capital, materials, energy, water, information, and so on – to produce the goods and services needed by society. Productivity is improved by creating more value per unit of input. The globalization of the economy has broadened significantly the ways in which value is created, and has expanded the range of options for inputs and outputs. A broader definition now exists that takes account of social and ecological impacts as both outputs and inputs in the productivity equation.

Globalization has had a great impact on the production systems of SMEs. Flexible production processes and structures are increasingly required to compete in very dynamic markets where product life is very short and discerning customers with higher purchasing power and more differentiated and international tastes are demanding much more product variety, higher quality and greater value for money. Hence, an enterprise's competitive advantage is increasingly found in improving the way it organizes and performs its sourcing, production and distribution activities.

The new production system consists of a network form of enterprise, where the product or service is produced and distributed by a network of enterprises, each contributing to the production and distribution according to their respective core competencies. Therefore, competitiveness now means the ability to constantly take the most advantageous position or niche in the rapidly changing market environment. This broader notion of productivity is opening up possibilities for SMEs that had greater difficulty competing on the traditional criteria of price, where economies of scale from larger production units typically made SMEs less competitive in all but niche markets. Even small firms can acquire a strong competitive position by creating and offering products and services of superior value to their customers concerning price, quality, distinctiveness, and so on. However, this competitive advantage requires better management and performance of the value chain of the enterprise. The changing structure of the production–distribution system shifts the focus of productivity improvement from looking exclusively at the organization's internal processes to examining the extended value chain, supply chain and networks of the organization. Hence partnerships not only within the enterprise but across the supply and distribution chains strengthen competitiveness.

Technology plays an important role in effective supply chain management. Firms that invest in the most up-to-date technology available are better able to manage production and the supply chain, to improve efficiency, develop new products and services and unleash the creativity and innovation of the workforce. New technologies can be costly and difficult to access for SMEs, but any firm can focus on making the most of locally available hard and soft technology. The benefits of upgraded technology can only be fully realized, however, if it is introduced together with new forms of work organization, continuous training and a learning environment. Labour–management partnership within the firm substantially affects the ability of enterprises to make the most of the best technology available.

With the rapid advance of technology and greater access to information, customer expectations are constantly changing and getting more demanding. Productivity improvement must now focus on value creation as a whole, and not just on minimization of inputs. Higher customer value is created when the products and services meet customer needs for utility, quality, diversity, timeliness, product support services, and so on. Innovation in these areas can be a key component of a competitive strategy for an SME to retain and expand market share and develop new markets. Workers know more than anyone how the product is made, how it can be made better, and how the related services can be improved; in a cooperative atmosphere they are a key source of information, creative ideas and solutions.

Environmental concerns are also shaping the current conception of productivity, drawing attention to "green production". Productivity improvement can play an important role in the preservation, rehabilitation and enhancement of the environment, through better use of energy, materials, water, solvents and other inputs. Here again, labour–management cooperation is essential for effective green production.

Globalization has also brought increasing expectations about the social performance of enterprises – often referred to as corporate citizenship. As pressure is exerted on multinationals to become more socially responsible, they in turn put pressure on their suppliers of all sizes. These pressures have spill-over effects on independent producers, even concerning local markets. There are growing expectations that enterprises of all sizes should have good social and ecological practices. The movement of people and capital has created numerous social issues for communities and countries, such as how to cope with the upheaval of communities, how to ensure that all people have equal access to education and employment, or what safety nets should exist to help people adjust to these rapid changes. However, SMEs often have unusually close ties to communities, and consequently are often involved in environmental and social issues in their community, regardless of any external pressures from buyers.

## Cooperation as a key source of enterprise competitiveness

An enterprise's source of productivity and competitiveness is capital – economic (plant, machines, trucks, etc.), human and social. Human and social capital enable a firm to make the best use of its economic capital. Making the best use of economic capital enables a firm to be profitable enough to acquire more economic capital, further improving its productivity and competitiveness. This virtuous circle is essential for firms to compete in a global economy with intense competition.

Human capital is embodied in workers and managers. It also exists along the supply chain and distribution channels. The knowledge and abilities of suppliers of inputs and people who get products to market have a significant impact on a firm's productivity, in particular for smaller firms which may have more dependent relationships with the other firms in its value chain. The human capital of the local community indirectly affects a firm's productivity because that is where its employees generally come from.

Many advanced systems of organizing and improving production require workers to assume more autonomy and responsibility, and require in particular that workers be proactive. To be proactive, workers need a sufficient level of skills to give them both the ability and the confidence to take on more responsibility. Workers with a variety of broader skills can adapt more quickly to change: when the job changes, such as introducing a new production method, or the job descriptions overlap more and require multi-tasking, workers with a variety of broader skills can get up to speed quicker; and when the firms need to adjust the workforce size, workers with a variety of broader skills can find another job more easily and therefore are less frightened of job loss.

Social capital is essential for a firm to make the most of its human capital. This is all the more so in small firms where relations are less formal and conditions of work generally are lower. Social capital is the means of motivating workers to make the most of their human capital. High levels of social capital enable workers and managers to carry out their job most effectively. Social capital is essential for building a sense of commitment to the enterprise as a whole which makes every employee want to do everything she or he can to get the job done, and done well.

Social capital is the social structures and networks that enable people to pursue shared objectives (Coleman, 1988). According to Dasgupta (2005),

Figure 1    The virtuous circle linking economic, human and social capital

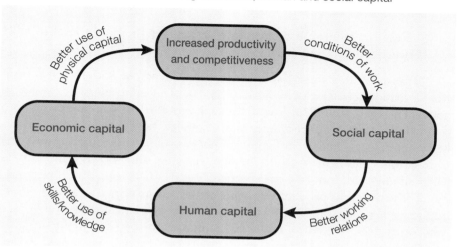

social capital is a component of total factor productivity: "There is no single object called social capital, there is a multitude of bits that together can be called social capital. Each bit reflects a set of interpersonal connections" (p. 6). These interpersonal connections are built on a sense of mutual benefit and shared interest in the outcome of cooperative behaviour. Researchers have become interested in studying social capital principally because it helps to explain why otherwise identical firms (in terms of physical capital, technology, human resources, access to markets, and so on) can differ substantially in productivity and competitiveness. High levels of social capital in a firm give it a competitive edge because it is able to operate with a substantially higher degree of commitment from workers, fewer administrative costs and in a way which is much more agile and proactive.

These interpersonal connections are termed "capital" because they have a value – they can be drawn upon to achieve an objective (for instance, obtaining employment for an individual, cleaning up the neighbourhood for a community, producing more effectively in teams) which would be either more costly or impossible to achieve without the interpersonal connections.

Social capital is built on trust. The key mechanisms for building trust are communication and cooperation. Trust, communication and cooperation are interdependent and mutually reinforcing:

•   The level of trust between workers and managers in an enterprise at any given moment heavily influences the willingness of workers and managers to communicate effectively with each other.

- The effectiveness of communication, in turn, determines how much workers and managers will cooperate to improve productivity.

- Success (or failure) in cooperating determines the future level of trust between workers and managers in the workplace.

Because of this interrelationship, the elements of social capital form either a virtuous circle, with high social capital, or a vicious one with low social capital. The vicious circle of low social capital is costly to an enterprise, both in terms of management resources and flexibility. Low social capital requires the owner-manager and other family members to constantly guard against acts to undermine the firm (waste, sabotage, slacking, and so on) which places increased demands on the entrepreneur's time. Consequently, low social capital directly harms productivity by diverting human capital away from more productive functions. In SMEs with very limited staff and already overworked owner-managers, the cost of low social capital can be particularly high.

Low social capital harms productivity by forcing managers to use controlling strategies which reduce the firm's flexibility and prevent it from making the best use of modern production management methods which rely on greater autonomy for teams of workers. Control requires more rigid and formal procedures, which leave the firm vulnerable in the face of changes in demand or increases in competition. A building structure must be solid, but if it is too rigid, it cannot withstand shocks such as strong winds and shifting ground. Likewise, an enterprise must also be solid yet able to absorb movement in markets through flexible production methods. Controlling management strategies based on lack of trust rob an enterprise of this valuable flexibility. Flexibility is especially important for team-based production methods. In an environment with high social capital, a work team can improve its production methods without seeking managerial approval first because management trusts the team's judgement and motives.

Low social capital also harms productivity because it obstructs the sharing of valuable information. Burt (1996) explains that high levels of trust in an enterprise bring both information access benefits (employees at all levels are more aware of issues and opportunities) and information timing benefits (they are aware earlier and able to act faster). Firms with low social capital cannot take full advantage of the valuable information their workers possess. Workers resist transmitting "bad news" if they fear being punished, or sharing "good news" if they believe that they will not benefit. In particular, they will not risk suggesting improvements unless they stand to gain if the suggestion proves useful, and do not stand to lose if it ultimately doesn't work out.

A low-trust environment where management constantly tells workers what to do can be very demotivating since the workers believe that the manager does not have confidence in their abilities. A work environment with high levels of trust is more productive because workers who are given more control over appropriate aspects of their job see themselves as important team members in the production process and are more engaged. Showing confidence in their abilities challenges workers to take more responsibility for their contribution to the production process.

Lastly, low social capital impairs the functioning of teams. Teams with high levels of trust are more open to discussion, develop more innovative and original solutions and solve their problems more effectively, and team members are less inclined to engage in behaviour which disrupts the work environment (Costa, 2003, p. 4). There is also evidence that the level of social capital influences how motivation is translated into group performance: in firms with high levels of social capital, team members focus more on joint efforts which yield higher performance; in firms with low social capital, motivation is transformed into individual efforts – so groups perform more poorly (Dirks, 1999).

In addition to direct effects, low social capital also harms productivity indirectly by diminishing the quantity and quality of human capital. Firms stuck in a low social capital trap have lower rates of investment in skills development, are less able to take advantage of the skills of their workforce, and have lower transmission of skills among workers. Schuller (2001, p. 4) explains: "Individuals and their human capital are not discrete entities that exist separately from the rest of the organization, or from other social units. The acquisition, deployment and effectiveness of skills depend crucially on the values and behavior patterns of the contexts within which these skills are expected to operate."

Social capital plays an important role in facilitating investment in human capital. Enterprises with low social capital have higher turnover rates – workers with other options prefer to work elsewhere and management is more likely to fire people rather than solve problems more constructively. Hence in such firms the rate of investment in skills development is lower because the firm expects that the worker will not be around for long enough to make most investment worthwhile. Likewise, workers are not willing to invest much effort in acquiring firm-specific skills which will be of little value to them when they leave the enterprise.

Social capital also plays an important role in ensuring that the training the firm invests in is put to use. Skills are of no value unless workers are sufficiently motivated to use them, and unless good communication channels exist within the firm to ensure the best match between the skills the firm needs in various positions and the skills its workforce possesses. Firms with higher social capital have more motivated workers (see for example Doeringer et al., 2002).

Furthermore, social capital facilitates the spread of skills and knowledge within a workforce. It has long been known that one of the most important channels for developing skills in an enterprise, particularly SMEs with limited resources to pay for formal training, is the informal transfer of knowledge in the workplace – occupational skills are learnt on the job, implicitly as well as consciously. Levin and Cross (2004, pp. 1477–1478) summarize the empirical findings concerning the impact of social capital on the development of human capital in an enterprise: people prefer to turn to other people rather than documents for information, even those with ready access to sources of information reported seeking information from colleagues significantly more than from impersonal sources; relationships have been found to be important for acquiring information, learning how to do one's work, making sense of ambiguous situations, and solving complex problems. "The trust literature . . . provides considerable evidence that trusting relationships lead to greater knowledge exchange: When trust exists, people are more willing to give useful knowledge . . . and are also more willing to listen to and absorb others' knowledge . . . By reducing conflicts and the need to verify information, trust also makes knowledge transfer less costly . . . These effects have been found at the individual and organizational levels of analysis in a variety of settings" (p. 1478).

Social capital also increases the quality of human capital. Much of the skills, knowledge and abilities workers possess is worth more in teams, due to their complementary nature. For instance, the value to a small enterprise of a product designer and production engineer is much higher when the designer and engineer work together to create a product than when they work in isolation – the product quality is likely to be higher, the turnaround time is generally shorter, and knowledge is shared in the cooperative process. In sum, the knowledge base of a workforce is richer as the level of trust, communication and cooperation increases.

Human and social capital have a symbiotic relationship in a firm. Social capital helps to cultivate and optimize the use of a firm's human capital. Human capital, in turn, facilitates the development of social capital. As the skills and knowledge base of workers increases, so does their confidence, making it easier for them to trust, communicate and cooperate. Furthermore, as Schuller (2001, p. 4) explains, investment in human capital can also be a means of investing in social capital because it strengthens networks and information flows.

## The link between cooperation and competitiveness

Today's global markets require firms to develop strategic partnerships to maintain and improve their competitive position. This is particularly true of small enterprises in developing countries where access to markets can be more challenging; hence, the growing importance of strategies to develop alliances, clusters and industries.

> Firms in communities with a large stock of social capital will . . . always have a competitive advantage to the extent that social capital [will] help reduce malfeasance, induce reliable information to be volunteered, cause agreements to be honoured, enable employees to share tacit information, and place negotiators on the same wave-length. This advantage gets even bigger when the process of globalization deepens the division of labour and thus augments the needs for coordination between and among firms. (Maskell, 1999, p. 7.)

Lall (2002, p. 10) reports that in order for enterprises to form an effective cluster, there needs to be "deliberate cooperation and joint action by cluster members to identify common problems and find and implement common solutions. This requires vision, trust, information sharing and coherence (along with continuing competition)." Without sufficient levels of social capital between firms, the effort involved in trying to strengthen a cluster may be more than it is worth. Social capital is also a necessary prerequisite for the transfer of best practices between firms in a cluster which makes possible the upgrading of the cluster as a whole; this is particularly important for the survival of small producers in a global economy.

The following chapter will look more closely at the forms of cooperation which exist in the enterprises studied.

# FORMS OF COMMUNICATION AND COOPERATION

# 3

Chapter 2 argued that labour–management cooperation is a vital part of a small firm's competitive strategy in global markets. In large part, the firms studied support this view, but not all. Taja Bakery in Nepal is an example of a firm which has been tremendously successful in expanding market share to date, despite the low level of cooperation in the enterprise; the firm pursues a controlling management strategy and instead invests heavily in good conditions of work to induce worker buy-in for increased productivity and innovation. Other enterprises, such as Maziwa in Kenya, demonstrate that even if management has a clear awareness of the need for cooperation, it may have little concrete knowledge of how exactly to build it.

The firms form a continuum (see figure 2), with some having relatively poor communication and cooperation, and others having developed relatively

Figure 2    Communication and cooperation: Relative positions of the firms studied

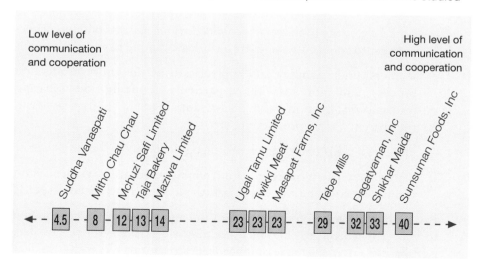

sophisticated management structures for promoting communication and cooperation.

Table 1 shows details of the ranking of the firms according to the following criteria:

- Stated commitment to developing labour–management cooperation. Indicators included expressions in mission statements, management guidelines, criteria for assessing the performance of managers, etc.

- Evidence that workers are viewed more as partners in the production process rather than as inputs. Indicators included respect for the rights of workers expressed in freedom of association, conditions of work which meet or exceed legal requirements, clearly expressed rules and procedures for deterring arbitrary or discriminatory management decisions, equality of opportunity and treatment, etc.

- Established mechanisms for communication and cooperation:

  - mechanisms for workers to express needs and concerns (trade union representation accepted, regular meetings between worker representatives and management, periodic direct access to top decision-makers, etc.)

  - mechanisms for workers to share opinions and suggestions (regular meetings, suggestion boxes, etc.)

- Investment in:

  - workers' skills (formal and on-the-job training, job rotation and enrichment, etc.)

  - workers' capacity to cooperate (confidence in their contribution, encouragement to contribute, support to workers wanting to contribute, etc.)

  - workers' understanding and appreciation of the entire production process and not just their particular contribution (sharing information beyond what is essential for a particular task, transparency, team production, etc.)

  - managers' skills (training, mentoring, guidelines)

  - managers' capacity to cooperate (training, mentoring, guidelines on facilitating cooperation, working with workers' representatives, etc.)

- Established incentives for communication and cooperation (responding to concerns where possible, incorporating suggestions where possible, gainsharing, criteria for assessing managers' performance, etc.)

Firms were scored on a scale of 0–3:

0    nothing exists for that category

1    some efforts, but relatively weak (e.g., a more passive approach, such as tolerating but not encouraging workers to express their views), pro forma efforts but without a constructive attitude (such as management-trade union councils which don't really function) or indicates a decline from past efforts

2    substantial efforts (such as actively cultivating cooperation, with some demonstrable effects), but some limitations (e.g., applies to permanent work force but not temporary or seasonal workers)

3    substantial efforts

The scoring was not based on precise measurements of absolute performance, but on relative performance. A firm which paid only slightly above the minimum wage but which was competing with firms which almost universally pay less than the minimum was assessed differently from one which paid the same as its local competitors.

Scoring was based on a range of factors, even for one particular indicator. For instance, an enterprise might have a strong policy concerning equality of opportunity between various ethnic groups, but be relatively weak on promoting gender equality. The score given for "non-discrimination" takes both factors into account.

Sometimes scoring also looks to circumstantial evidence to evaluate claims, in some cases even when there is no conflict of opinion between workers and management. For instance, how does one know for certain the reason why a firm does not have a trade union? Is it that, although management respects the right to organize, workers genuinely do not want to organize, or because they are made to understand that management does not support the organization of workers? Workers may not be able to state freely their views on whether management respects their right to organize, so the cases were examined for evidence of consistency between claims about behaviour and actual behaviour. A score of 0.5 indicates that doubts existed about the claims, although they were not contradicted by the workers.

Lastly, it is important to keep in mind that this study looks at performance at only one point in time. Although interviews brought out some changes over time within firms, which are occasionally mentioned in the text, no baseline study was conducted which could allow for a more accurate assessment.

Table 1   Scoring of firms: Indicators of labour–management cooperation

| Indicators | Name of enterprise | | | | | | | | | | | |
|---|---|---|---|---|---|---|---|---|---|---|---|---|
| | Dagatyaman Seafoods | Masapat Farms | Maziwa | Mchuzi Safi | Mitho Chau Chau Foods | Shikhar Maida | Suddha Vanaspati | Sumsuman Foods | Taja Bakery | Tebe Mills | Twikki Meat | Ugali Tamu |
| **Stated commitment** | 3 | 1 | 1 | 2 | 1 | 3 | 0 | 3 | 1 | 3 | 2 | 3 |
| **Evidence of partnership approach** | | | | | | | | | | | | |
| Respect right to form union and bargain collectively | 2 | 1 | 0 | 1 | 1 | 3 | 0.5 | 1 | 0 | 1 | 1 | 2 |
| Conditions of work | 2 | 2 | 2 | 2 | 1 | 3 | 1 | 3 | 2 | 2 | 2 | 3 |
| Non-arbitrary management | 3 | 1 | 1 | 1 | 1 | 3 | 1 | 3 | 1 | 2 | 2 | 2 |
| Non-discrimination policy | 0 | 0 | 1 | 2 | 0 | 0 | 0 | 1 | 0 | 2 | 2 | 1 |
| **Mechanisms for communication** | | | | | | | | | | | | |
| Worker needs and concerns | 2 | 1 | 1 | 1 | 1 | 2 | 0 | 3 | 1 | 3 | 2 | 2 |
| Worker suggestions | 3 | 2 | 2 | 0 | 0 | 2 | 0 | 3 | 1 | 3 | 2 | 2 |
| **Investment in:** | | | | | | | | | | | | |
| Worker skills | 2 | 2 | 1 | 1 | 1 | 2 | 1 | 3 | 1 | 1 | 1 | 1 |
| Worker capacity for cooperation | 2 | 2 | 1 | 0 | 0 | 2 | 0 | 3 | 1 | 2 | 1 | 1 |
| Worker understanding of entire production process | 3 | 2 | 0 | 0 | 0 | 2 | 0 | 3 | 1 | 3 | 1 | 1 |
| Management skills | 2 | 2 | 2 | 1 | 1 | 2 | 1 | 3 | 1 | 1 | 1 | 2 |
| Management capacity for cooperation | 2 | 2 | 1 | 0 | 0 | 2 | 0 | 3 | 1 | 1 | 1 | 1 |
| **Incentives to communicate and cooperate** | | | | | | | | | | | | |
| Respond to needs/concerns | 1 | 1 | 1 | 1 | 1 | 2 | 0 | 3 | 1 | 2 | 2 | 2 |
| Gainsharing | 2 | 2 | 1 | 0 | 0 | 3 | 0 | 2 | 1 | 2 | 2 | 1 |
| Criteria for assessing management performance | 3 | 2 | 0 | 0 | 0 | 2 | 0 | 3 | 0 | 1 | 1 | 1 |
| Total | 32 | 23 | 14 | 12 | 8 | 33 | 4.5 | 40 | 13 | 29 | 23 | 23 |

The extent and forms of labour–management cooperation in small enterprises is expected to differ from the partnership in large enterprises. Studies of participatory productivity and quality improvement systems, such as Total Quality Management (TQM), show some particular characteristics of SMEs that influence the application of participatory labour-management practices (Tannock et al., 2002, and table 2).

Table 2    Major management implications of characteristics of small enterprises

| Observed characteristic | Implications for management styles and practices |
|---|---|
| Close link between the personality and behaviour of the entrepreneur and the small business | High degree of centralization<br>Personalized management style<br>Strong personal loyalty considerations<br>Lack of succession plans<br>Shortage of time for management and other tasks |
| Close link of the small enterprise to the family and immediate community | Strong influence of the family and community culture<br>Informal approach to personnel recruitment and development<br>Informal approach to management control |
| Small size of business operations | Simple and flexible processes and systems<br>Multi-functional role of the entrepreneur-manager<br>Informal communication and record keeping<br>Close relationship with the workers<br>Strong reliance on on-the-job training<br>Easier integration between policy and practice<br>Shortage of management and other resources |
| Narrow financial resource base | Over-riding goal of reducing risk through retaining control<br>Stress on operational issues of management<br>Preoccupation with finance as a functional decision-making area<br>Limited strategic planning<br>Focus on short-term results<br>Lower investment in social capital |
| Limited internal technological base | Dependence on knowledge and know-how of particular individuals<br>Need for continuous technology acquisition and transfusion from the outside |

Source: Adapted from Meredith et al., 1982. Adaptation first published in Tolentino, 1997.

This next sections look more closely at what forms of communication and cooperation exist in the enterprises studied.

# Communication

Communication and the flow of information can be unilateral or bilateral, or in some firms a mixture, depending on the issues involved. At one end of the spectrum, some firms have no effective forms of in-house communication, with no information flowing from workers to managers and a highly restricted flow of information from managers to workers. For example, Taja Bakery has no mechanism for consultation and only highly limited communication. Instead, it follows a very paternalistic approach to management with a heavy emphasis on unilateral communication. In order to compensate for the low level of social capital such a management style generates, it also depends heavily on welfare as the basis of building trust in the enterprise, providing workers with dormitories for night shifts, good wages and benefits, hot meals, health insurance and savings accounts, but no voice. Such mitigating efforts have helped the company to build some sense of loyalty to the enterprise, in terms of very low turnover of staff, but it has not contributed much to cooperation – workers do not resist changes imposed by management; but neither do they share information, take initiatives, or propose improvements.

In the most extreme example among the firms studied, Suddha Vanaspati has too little trust to even follow this paternalism/welfare model. In this firm there is no communication except for management occasionally to inform workers of decisions taken. Management has tried to introduce a welfare committee to build some basis of trust between workers and managers, but the effort failed. Consequently, there are no ideas or initiatives coming from workers which could help to turn the ailing firm around.

At the other end of the spectrum, some firms have sought very actively to foster bilateral communication, often using a variety of channels. For instance, Sumsuman Foods has a policy whereby ad hoc discussions can be initiated by either workers or managers; and management has instituted annual one-on-one talks between the president and every worker, where workers can raise any issue.

Some firms have no fixed intervals for meetings. Tebe Mills is one such firm which is now considering institutionalizing labour–management discussions, as there is a value to gathering together on a regular basis, regardless of whether a specific issue needs to be addressed.

Some firms have instituted meetings at all levels. For instance, Twikki Meat holds monthly labour–management meetings, periodic management–supervisor meetings which allow some worker input; and daily production management meetings with supervisors and workers to plan output and address production issues. In addition, workers meet periodically to address common concerns and share ideas. Workers can request that the managing director attend these meetings when they want to present an idea directly to top management.

Some firms have implemented a mix of ad hoc and set intervals for dialogue. As we have seen above, Sumsuman Foods holds ad hoc meetings which can be initiated by either workers or managers. But the president also holds annual one-on-one talks with every individual worker; and management and workers meet regularly to discuss production issues, conditions of work and grievances. Masapat Farms holds monthly staff assemblies, monthly management meetings where workers can communicate information and concerns through their supervisors, and weekly meetings between staff and department heads.

In one case, there was no institutionalized internal communications because it exists at another level. Shikhar Maida does not have a labour relations committee at the enterprise level because the district level tripartite committee has decided to establish a regional labour relations committee. Although such a body is helpful in many respects, the firm is planning to form a joint welfare committee focusing on the distribution of funds set aside for worker activities and benefits, in part in order to establish an in-house platform for more frequent worker–management dialogue.

However, institutionalized communication does not guarantee dialogue and two-way flow of information. Taja Bakery has weekly staff meetings, but the workers – all young women recruited for their tendency to be more passive than male or older female workers – do not actively participate, share information or offer ideas.

In several of the firms studied, workers had direct access to top management where they could communicate their ideas and concerns without any filters from middle management. At Taja Bakery top management attends the workers' staff meeting at the end of each month, which gives workers the opportunity to raise any issues, including personnel problems. The managing director of Tebe Mills maintains an open-door policy for workers to discuss with her ideas, concerns, issues concerning production, conditions of work or grievances, as well as outside issues which directly or indirectly affect performance (mainly financial difficulties and problems balancing work and family obligations). Top management at Twikki Meat has a similar policy. Sumsuman Foods and Dagatyaman both have a policy where workers can discuss any issue with senior management at any time, although they are encouraged to speak to their supervisor in the first instance when appropriate. And Masapat Farms has a policy of the president communicating face-to-face with staff members whenever possible rather than through communication channels and written communiqués.

The subjects most commonly addressed between workers and managers in enterprises with systems for bilateral communication include organization of production, conditions of work, grievances and conflict resolution. As already mentioned, some enterprises invite workers to discuss personal matters affecting their performance in the workplace. Tebe Mills and Sumsuman Foods both use 360-degree feedback on performance appraisal where workers can provide feedback to their immediate supervisors and management on their performance.

On the specific issue of productivity, about half the enterprises studied had no mechanism for communication. At one extreme, some firms viewed production and productivity improvement as an area under the exclusive control of management, and did not solicit information or ideas from workers. For instance, management at Mitho Chau Chau exercised direct personal control of all facets of production on a daily basis, with excessively centralized decision-making and no flow of information to workers on production issues, apart from simple instructions narrowly related to each worker's job description. Firms such as Suddha Vanaspati communicated more, but only to inform workers of decisions concerning productivity already taken by management.

In the middle were firms such as Taja Bakery, which held staff meetings concerning productivity issues; but such meetings could only be initiated by management, and the flow of information coming from workers was limited. Some firms had consultation mechanisms by virtue of a particular productivity improvement or quality control system they applied in the production process rather than as a consequence of management commitment to fostering communication per se. For instance, the only communication mechanisms existing at Ugali Tamu were due to the requirements of a meat-exporting quality control certification system, Hazard Analysis and Critical Control Point (HACCP), which requires extensive worker involvement in decision-making at critical junctures of the production process.

At the other extreme were firms such as Sumsuman Foods, which holds morning staff meetings devoted in part to discussing productivity issues among all workers and managers together, with 15-minute videos shown every other day on particular issues such as safety and health, followed by discussion. It also holds quarterly thematic worker–manager discussions with outside resource persons on various productivity and management issues.

One firm felt it was particularly important to foster communication among workers concerning productivity, to share knowledge and experiences. At Tebe Mills consultation teams are based on functional groups, to discuss issues among themselves and share experiences and knowledge, as a form of ongoing on-the-job learning. These same teams are the basis for discussing and proposing solutions to issues related to conditions of work, benefits and grievances, with the idea of linking these issues to productivity and rooting them in the relationships fostered through communication among team members.

Festivals, picnics, and other social events which include the entire staff create opportunities for further interaction and trust-building between management and workers. For instance, Shikhar Maida held an annual picnic for staff and their families, as well as a feast with all staff during the local religious festival. Sumsuman Foods sponsored voluntary Bible study sessions 3 days per week, Mass for the staff once a month, and an annual retreat before the Easter holy week. Even enterprises with otherwise poor communications mechanisms sponsored such activities, owing to their strong ties to the communities in which they operated.

Lastly, one firm, Sumsuman Foods, additionally built social capital between workers and managers through a monthly newsletter to which both contributed and by sponsoring sports activities.

## Cooperation

Good labour–management communication is the foundation for cooperation on improving productivity, monitoring quality, diversifying products, and retaining and expanding market share. Regular communication and interaction, in which each side listens to the other's ideas, concerns and problems, helps to develop the trust which is needed for cooperation: for managers to have sufficient confidence in workers to delegate decision-making to them, and for workers to feel sufficiently confident in management, and in themselves, to take a more proactive role and assume more responsibility for productivity improvement. The firms studied show a flow (see box 2) between the following components of cooperation:

1   in the first instance, a management commitment to developing effective bilateral communication;

2   then workers' willingness to share information, leading to a good bilateral flow of information;

3   subsequently, as mutual trust and confidence develop, management becomes more willing to delegate decision-making authority to workers; and

4   lastly, workers demonstrate an increased willingness and enthusiasm to cooperate in productivity improvement and product development.

For instance, management at Twikki Meat has made effective communication a priority, with positive results. Management has sufficient

Box 2    The impact of good communication and cooperation on productivity and competitiveness: Tebe Mills

Tebe Mills has an informal but extensive labour–management communication and cooperation system. There are few scheduled meetings, but labour–management discussions are frequently held, and can be convened on the initiative of either side. The human resources officer is considering establishing fixed intervals for meetings between labour and management. The managing director also operates an open-door policy where workers can raise not only issues pertaining to the workplace, but also personal issues which may have an impact on their performance in the workplace.

Any complaints received from customers concerning quality are discussed between management and workers and anyone can propose a solution. Workers and management jointly develop action plans to address concerns and problems involving salaries, absenteeism, health and safety, transportation for night shift workers, and fraud.

Workers are empowered to replace any non-performing team member without approval from management, although the replaced worker can appeal the decision to management. Workers are responsible for deciding whether the quality of the inputs and outputs is adequate, and are authorized to take action, such as rejecting a shipment of grain without management approval.

Workers have cooperated in productivity improvements by:

• agreeing to more flexible working arrangements for large and rush orders

• providing input into their performance appraisals through initial self-appraisal, which makes workers more conscious of management's perspective

Workers have contributed to improvements by:

• proactively reporting that the sealing machine was not working properly so that it was fixed rapidly

• taking the initiative on improving the mixing of product textures, which they felt was not adequate

• proposing solutions for smoothing production peaks and lulls

• suggesting improvements in the compensation plan to better reflect the contributions of workers

• proposing that management produce animal feed from the waste material produced, an idea that the firm is now developing

In addition to taking these suggestions on board, management has shown flexibility in accommodating worker preferences, for instance in the following adaptations:

- paydays were moved to before weekends on the suggestion of workers

- adjusting the compensation package in response to worker suggestions

Some accommodations of worker needs have led directly to productivity improvements. For instance, workers complained about having to wear protective masks, a practice that impairs their productivity and is particularly uncomfortable in the heat. In response, management suggested that some of the processes be automated to eliminate dust so that the workers would no longer need to wear protective masks. The workers agreed to this suggestion, and the automation has increased productivity.

confidence in workers to substantially involve them in operational decision-making, including letting them decide how much overtime they would like to work and allowing each team of workers to deal in the first instance with its internal discipline issues the way it thinks appropriate. Workers in turn have initiated process and product changes, which have been accepted by management, including:

- changing the packaging with considerable cost savings;

- switching to more flexible working hours to enable the enterprise to respond more quickly to large orders and reduce production delays;

- developing ideas for three new products;

- recommending that a worker be designated for production of biltong (beef cured in a particular way) which improved both productivity and quality; and

- suggesting improvements in wages and benefits which did not increase the wage bill for the enterprise.

Management at Twikki has also benefited from a high number of worker referrals of new recruits, and the relatively low turnover rate; these have reduced recruitment and retention costs for the firm. Similarly, other firms which have invested in cultivating cooperation have also benefited from lower staff turnover. For instance, Taja Bakery has an exceptionally low 2-3 per cent annual turnover rate; and Tebe Mill's rate is only slightly higher.

In contrast, Mitho Chau Chau Foods follows a very paternalistic model of management. There is no commitment on the part of management to developing effective communication; on the contrary, even the flow of information from management to workers is highly restricted. Management shows little trust or confidence in workers, and interaction is too restricted for them to develop an alternative understanding of what the workers could contribute. Not surprisingly, workers have no reason to believe that their contribution beyond the minimum required to keep their jobs would benefit anyone but management, and hence have not contributed to any improvements in the enterprise.

Sumsuman Foods provides a particularly clear example of the link between communication and cooperation for improving productivity. The human resources manager conducted a diagnosis of employee perceptions of the company. This exercise in actively listening to the views of workers led to changes in the benefits and programmes for workers which were more appropriate to their needs. Based on their increased trust and confidence in management brought about by this exercise, workers in turn changed their attitude and commitment to productivity increases. As a consequence, management was able to introduce TQM (total quality management) and 5S (a methodology from Japan for organizing the manufacturing workplace by clearing up unnecessary clutter, organizing the work space, cleaning, standardizing through perpetual cleaning, and self-discipline in adhering to standards) into their production systems, which it had tried to introduce before without success. This change has lead to an increase in productivity and product quality, and also helped to eliminate the filing of formal grievance complaints.

One of the most important means of fostering communication and cooperation is gain-sharing through productivity incentives for individual or team performance: bonuses paid based on profits, investing productivity gains in worker benefits, training or amenities, and so on. Gain-sharing is a key means for management to cultivate trust with workers, by showing that they recognize and reward workers' contribution to productivity improvements. Workers are inclined to contribute less, or not at all, to productivity improvement if they do not receive any benefit.

Six of the firms studied had some form of gain-sharing. For instance, at Shikhar Maida workers suggested shifting to off-peak production to save energy costs. Management has accepted this idea and distributes the monthly savings from the lower energy bill to the workers. Dagatyaman provides a range of incentives to workers, including casual workers, to communicate ideas and concerns regarding productivity, and to express grievances. Masapat Farms provides incentives for productivity improvement, linked to both output and sales, but does not consult with workers on the particular incentives; this may diminish their effectiveness. Sumsuman Foods provides an interesting example of how management has used recognition to motivate workers to help improve productivity and quality (see box 3).

However, some firms studied did not fully appreciate the importance of gain-sharing. For instance, at Ugali Tamu management did not have a system

Box 3   The value of recognition for improving quality

A particularly important psychological aspect of gain-sharing is the appreciation and public recognition of workers' contribution to productivity improvements.

Sumsuman Foods has developed a Quality Improvement Project (QIP). The objective is to involve workers more closely in management decision-making. Although focused primarily on quality improvement, workers can also suggest improvements in design, work environment, safety and health, disease prevention and other aspects of production. The company realizes that innovations are easily copied, and therefore continuous innovation is important to retain a competitive edge in the market.

All proposed improvements go to the Quality Satisfaction Team, which is composed of a group of six workers who report directly to the president. The team is responsible for reviewing all proposals and choosing those which it considers worthwhile and feasible to implement. It assesses the impact and effectiveness of selected proposals and recommends those which are positively assessed to become standard operating procedure in the enterprise. For those suggestions which present some difficulties, the team works with the person making the suggestion to see if it can be refined and improved rather than simply rejected.

So far, seven QIP ideas have been put forward by workers. Of these seven, four have been implemented and three have been submitted for further review to see if the cost of implementation could be brought down. Areas of improvement include altering the way of cleaning equipment so as to save on hot water, and improving product quality by raising the temperature for cooking the product.

The person who originated the suggestion is invited to present it to workers and managers at a 5S programme meeting. Workers whose ideas are accepted are given cash rewards and are publicly recognized for their contribution. There is also an annual award given for the best QIP of the year.

Inviting worker suggestions and providing rewards and recognition provides a way for workers to showcase their creativity and innovativeness, and for building worker commitment. And placing a team of workers in charge of assessing the merits of each suggestion encourages workers to assume more responsibility for assessing and implementing improvements. In such a system, workers are invited to view the company more from a managerial perspective, and managers are encouraged to recognize the contribution workers can make to improving productivity and competitiveness. In the process of developing a better understanding of the perspectives and concerns of the other, workers and managers are able to develop better communication and cooperation.

of gain-sharing even though it was critical to the business to have good communication and cooperation for HACCP certification.

Although gain-sharing is an important means of drawing a clear link between communication and cooperation and productivity improvement, broader conditions of work and management practices concerning recruitment, promotion, handling of grievances, and so on, play a much more fundamental role in helping to build social capital in an enterprise. Chapter 4 will look more closely at the link between management practices and labour–management cooperation.

# HUMAN RESOURCES MANAGEMENT PRACTICES AND THEIR IMPACT ON THE DEVELOPMENT OF COOPERATION

# 4

Human resources management (HRM) practices have a fundamental affect on management's ability to develop labour–management cooperation in an enterprise. The way in which an enterprise recruits workers, its level of investment in skills development and ensuring a safe workplace, the wages and benefits it provides, and the manner in which management resolves grievances all send a very strong signal to workers about how much their contribution is valued, and serve as the primary motivation for workers in turn to increase their contribution to improving the competitive position of the enterprise.

## Earlier studies on human resources management and employment relations practices in SMEs

Until the recent outpouring of literature on the employment relationship in SMEs, most research in this area had focused on large organizations, even though research findings suggest that employment practices in the latter have limited application in small firms.[3] Not only has the increased attention to the nature of the employment relationship in smaller firms highlighted such differences, but considerable attention has also been focused on the extent of the voice mechanism and the implications for organizational and employment rights, as well as the role of workers in organizational performance.

The literature on human resources management identifies a series of normative employment practices which are regularly described as "strategic" or "best practice" concepts that are integral to or align with overall business strategy (Guest, 2001; Marchington and Grugulis, 2000; Boxall, 1996; Huselid, 1995). Among the key human resources practices commonly identified are employee participation, harmonious relations, discipline and grievance

---

[3] For a fairly comprehensive recent assessment of the growing interest in the human resources and employment relationship in small firms, see Wilkinson, 1999.

procedures, flexibility in the employment relationship, performance and reward systems, selection processes and internal promotion (Boselie and Jansen, 2001) However, much of the literature is based on large organizations (Guest, 1997; Wood, 1996; Capelli and Crocker-Hefter, 1996).

Doubts exist about the applicability to small firms of research focusing on larger enterprises, and there is growing interest in exploring these concepts and practices in SMEs (Horstman, 1999; Bacon et al., 1996). But evidence shows that these practices exist in small firms to varying extents, and seem to have an effect on enterprise performance (Bacon et al., 1996). However, such studies tend to focus only on enterprises without unions (Ramaswamy and Schiphorst, 2000; Beaumont, 1995, Guest and Conway, 1999; Abbott, 1993). The issue therefore is not the relevance of the human resources activities in small firms, but the context in which they are practised and how.

## Formality of human resources policy and practices

Several studies have shown that one of the distinguishing characteristics of human resources management practice in small firms is the concern for informality and flexibility for a whole range of practices (Matlay, 1999; Ritchie, 1993). However, the cases demonstrate that nonetheless small firms often develop some degree of formality in order to promote transparent, predictable and overall more professional management.

Six of the 12 enterprises studied have what could be referred to as a formal human resources policy, to the extent that some employment relationship issues are formally written and implemented. However, there are differences in detail and degree of formalization, often depending on the size of the workforce, the business environment and the functions of the owner/manager. Some of the firms operating informally appear to be in the process of transition to the adoption of formal human resources policy.

The most common evidence of formal human resources management policy is the introduction of some form of employee handbook, as exists in several of the enterprises covered in this study. In these, the employee handbook typically provides guidance to workers on the terms and basic conditions of employment, employees' rights and obligations, company rights and obligations to the workers. It also sets out the procedures for recruitment, probation and discipline. In these cases, the key objective of human resources management is to provide a new worker with a good orientation and to clarify expectations on both sides. However, it is not clear from the cases whether any effort is made to monitor the effectiveness of the human resources management policy, as often happens in larger organizations.

The recruitment of a personnel manager seems to be a catalyst in the transition to more formal structures. In Maziwa there has been a gradual shift in orientation towards professional management of the enterprise, with the appointment of a general manager, two line managers and two supervisors. Subsequently, in response to a complaint by senior workers that their wages did not reflect their contribution to the enterprise, the new general manager developed a written compensation plan. Similarly, in Sumsuman Foods and Tebe Mills the owner-managers have over time ceded most operational functions to line managers, allowing the former to concentrate on strategic business issues. In both firms, the recruitment of a human resources specialist resulted in the latter taking over most of the operational human resources functions. In Sumsuman Foods the personnel manager has introduced a formal performance management system as the basis for reward and compensation.

At the same time, despite the adoption of a formal human resources policy, or movement towards it, the firms have generally maintained a certain degree of flexibility and informality in dealing with employment issues. For example, when dealing with discipline issues, the firms studied rarely referred to predetermined rules but instead treated every case as it arose, to leave managers a lot of leeway in responding most appropriately in a particular situation.

For many SMEs, the choice to remain relatively flexible is due in part to an unstable business environment, or simply the fear of the unknown, which makes the owner reluctant to alter the status quo. For instance, Suddha Vanaspati, a ghee manufacturer in Nepal, has experienced intense competition as a result of a change in import policy for its main export market and consequently has been reluctant to set up a formal system out of concern for operational costs. In contrast, management at Taja Bakery, a successful enterprise serving the local market in the same country and sub-sector, is contemplating a formal system which would include a recruitment policy and a career development plan, to enable the firm to retain committed staff and to develop rules for the disengagement of non-performing workers.

## Recruitment policies and practices

For most firms there is no written recruitment policy as such, but there appears to be a deliberate choice to recruit workers from the community in which the enterprise operates. Recruitment tends to occur informally, drawing on networks of family members, friends and neighbours for staffing the enterprise, particularly in positions requiring unskilled and semi-skilled workers. In view of the limited scope for skilled and professional personnel in most of the small firms studied, it appears that more formalized recruitment strategies are rarely needed. This confirms the findings by researchers such as Carroll et al. (1999).

Using local networks has numerous advantages. Search costs are reduced or eliminated when the enterprise relies on employees to scout out prospective applicants, provide information on the position, and do much of the pre-screening of applicants. Local networks provide a more flexible and quicker means of filling vacancies, which is particularly attractive for small enterprises where recruitment is based on immediate need rather than a longer-term staffing strategy.

Recruiting workers based on the personal recommendations of current employees also has the benefit of reinforcing the bond of loyalty, trust and commitment to organizational goals. Workers referred by their family or friends are able to adapt more quickly due to the information and assistance provided by their connections already working in the firm. They are also under greater peer pressure to perform well, since any failure will reflect poorly on the worker who recommended the new recruit. A referral by the employee also serves as a sign of appreciation for the job and working conditions of the employer; likewise, hiring the person referred is a sign that the manager trusts the judgement of the employee making the referral. In other words, drawing on the network of employees and community fosters commitment and loyalty among new recruits and reinforces these attitudes in existing employees.

It should be noted, however, that building on existing ties also brings with it the risk that the work relationships may sour if the personal ties do, and that in any case ties that are too close can complicate operations within the firm. For instance, management at Twikki Meat encourages current employees to suggest friends or neighbours for employment, but it does not recruit their relatives because that could create family squabbles or problems, which could have an adverse effect on productivity and harmony in the workplace. Furthermore, relying too heavily on local ties can cause a firm to be insular and inadvertently promote discrimination against workers who do not have ties to the firm. Nonetheless, in the case of the small firms studied, the benefits of informal recruitment mechanisms seemed to outweigh the disadvantages.

Although a community network strategy has many advantages, the main justification given by most enterprise owners for depending on workers for recruitment was their sense of obligation to contribute to the social and economic development of the community in which they operate. For instance, the owner-manager of Tebe Mills informed us that she felt she had a moral obligation to contribute to her community through the employment of youth. This sense of responsibility towards the community is also the driving force for the recruitment policy of Dagatyaman. The firm recruits most of its core and casual workers from the local community of Cordova, which accounted for 70 per cent of total workers.

In most cases it is the owner-managers themselves who recruit workers, although in a few cases, such as the firms Tebe Mills and Dagatyaman, line managers or supervisors can recruit casual workers, or recommend to the owner-manager the recruitment of temporary workers or the transfer to the core permanent cadre. Consequently, such recruitment guidelines as exist usually reflect the preferences and cultural beliefs of the owner-manager of the business. For example, the recruitment policy of Masapat Farms bans the recruitment of smokers and people who drink alcoholic beverages.

Although recruitment is based on shorter-term need, the small enterprises studied often indicated a longer-term retention strategy. For instance, in Mchuzi Safi the goal of the recruitment and termination policy is to maintain a 4 per cent involuntary attrition rate and zero per cent voluntary attrition – the owners do not want good workers to leave, but they want to replace the least productive workers each year with more productive and motivated people. An owner explained:

> At one point, the voluntary attrition rate was 8 per cent. I started calling every employee who wanted to leave into my office to discuss the reason why. After our talk most of them decided to stay. Now the voluntary attrition rate is less than 1 per cent. They just wanted to know that somebody cared.

Most of the firms use an internal labour market to help reconcile the desire to retain good workers with the greater use of non-permanent contracts. Recruiting from pools of seasonal, temporary or casual workers already familiar with the enterprise helps the small enterprise to ensure a stable workforce of experienced workers who are motivated by the prospect of promotion to more desirable posts. For example, in Dagatyaman two categories of staff exist – core staff totalling 50, and seasonal staff of 150 workers. The seasonal workers accept seasonal employment contracts because they provide a reliable source of income, and because vacancies for permanent positions are filled from the pool of seasonal workers. Mitho Chau Chau Foods also fills permanent posts from its pool of temporary workers, while casual labourers have the possibility to move up to the relatively more stable temporary posts. Internal labour markets also make it possible for small enterprises to invest in basic training for non-permanent workers. At Masapat Farms, where business increases by about 30 to 50 per cent during the Christmas season, a large number of casual workers are hired as trainees for a period of 3 months on the understanding that they will be rehired for future seasons provided they are available and fit. Workers are interested in participating because the company recruits its core workforce from this pool of seasonal workers.

## Staffing policies and practices

The percentage of women workers varied widely across firms, even within the same country. However, men uniformly dominated management-level positions, and with minor exceptions, women were concentrated in the lower ranks. Table 3 shows the number of women and men working in each of the enterprises surveyed, as well as the number of permanent, casual, and temporary workers (see table 3).

The recruitment strategy in many enterprises was to target young workers, in particular women. Various reasons were given for this, including employers' perception that female workers are more productive and more reliable than male workers because of the structure of the economy and labour force. In Botswana, for example, male workers in primarily rural settings alternate between industrial employment and agricultural labour, and therefore tend to remain in a particular post for shorter periods of time.

However, the prevalence of female workers in the food-processing sub-sector also owes much to cultural stereotypes of women, in particular young women, as more dependable and hardworking, more adaptable to authority than male workers, and less confrontational or aggressive. For instance, management at Taja Bakery took pride in deviating from the tradition of hiring mainly or exclusively male workers, and instead recruited young, unmarried women, who constitute 50 per cent of the 276 workers and account for virtually all the production workforce, with the more experienced women workers serving as supervisors.

A large proportion of the workforce in the small firms studied is in non-standard employment (described by those interviewed as either contract, casual or temporary work) owing to the seasonal nature of the work. For instance, at Dagatyaman Seafoods in the Philippines, 150 of the 200 workers, or 75 per cent, are temporary workers, and only 50 are permanent "core" workers. At Mitho Chau Chau Foods there are 170 "regular" workers and 300 non-regular casual labourers. Of the regular workers, only 10 have permanent employment contracts, leaving the large majority in temporary employment status. Of the 50 women employees, only 3 have permanent contracts. Those with permanent contracts work mainly in administrative functions.

The use of contingent and temporary contracts makes recruitment of young people more likely, as more experienced workers look for more stable employment. Most of the workers engaged in the enterprises studied are in the 20-to-early-30s age bracket. At Dagatyaman, for example, while the core workers were generally in their 30s and 40s, the vast majority of casual workers (about 80 per cent) were in their 20s. At Sumsuman Foods the average age of workers was 26 years, while the average for management supervisory cadres was 32.5 years.

Table 3     Composition of the workforce in SMEs studied

| Country | Male[1] | Female | Core[2] permanent | Temporary[3] | Casual[4] | Total |
|---|---|---|---|---|---|---|
| **Botswana** | | | | | | |
| Tebe Mills | 60 | 60 | 97 | – | 23 | 120 |
| Twikki Meat | 34 | 31 | 65 | – | – | 65 |
| **Kenya** | | | | | | |
| Maziwa | 19 | 7 | 26 | – | 8 | 34 |
| Mchuzi Safi | 39 | 51 | 81 | – | 9 | 90 |
| Ugali Tamu | 17 | 3 | 20 | – | 24 | 44 |
| **Philippines** | | | | | | |
| Dagatyaman Seafood | 40 | 160 | 50 | 150 | – | 200 |
| Masapat Farms | 156 | 40 | 101 | 51 | 44 (trainees) | 196 |
| Sumsuman Foods | 35 | 15 | 50 | – | – | 50 |
| **Nepal** | | | | | | |
| Mitho Chau Chau Foods | 120 | 50 | 10 | 160 | 300 | 470 |
| Shikhar Maida | 77 | 3 | 61 | – | 19 | 80 |
| Suddha Vanaspati | 83 | 2 | 85 | – | 100–200 | 185–285 |
| Taja Bakery | 136 | 140 | 276 | – | – | 276 |

[1] Breakdown by sex may be of either all workers in the enterprise, or certain categories, depending on whether temporary and casual workers are consistently of the same sex.

[2] Workers who are on fixed-term employment contracts with the employer and who constitute the primary workforce in the firm.

[3] Workers who are engaged for defined periods and are not on fixed-term employment contracts with the firm.

[4] Workers employed on a day-to-day basis with irregular employment contracts.

Owners of small firms generally opt for contingent workers in an attempt to ensure flexibility in their use of labour due to the seasonal nature of the work and to enable them to respond to uncertainties in the economic environment. However, this form of flexibility comes at the price of increased instability in labour relations and hence lower performance of the enterprise. Engaging contingent workers makes workers' solidarity, or forming a union, an almost impossible task, because such workers rarely see the need for workers' solidarity or to join the union, leaving the enterprise without a formal partner to work with on systematically improving productivity and competitiveness. Contingent workers often do not see themselves as part of "the family" because they have no sense of attachment to the organization. In this context they may have no real commitment to organizational goals. Furthermore, contingent employment, particularly in small firms, generally involves substandard employment conditions because casual workers do not enjoy many of the conditions of service offered to regular workers, or even the minimum conditions mandated by law.

The staffing policy is directly linked to the prosperity of the enterprise, and explains why several of the firms studied prefer informal human resources policies, such as the recruitment of non-permanent or contingent workers. The experience of Ugali Tamu illustrates this reality. The firm rapidly expanded total employment to 70 permanent workers. Exports were 95 per cent of its products, mostly to the United States and Canada. However, in 1976 exports plummeted and the percentage of permanent employees fell drastically. Management's goal now is to remain small, and to concentrate on retaining local market share.

## Training and development

There is growing recognition in SMEs of the benefits of training and development to business success, even where operational and environmental constraints limit investment in human resources or where there is no formal training and development policy (Loan-Clarke et al., 1999). In most of the firms in this study, skills requirements are very simple, which accounts both for the relatively limited scope of the training and development function and also the informality of such activity. At the same time, while investment in training is limited in the firms in this study, there is nevertheless a perceived positive effect of training on employee effectiveness and organizational performance. This linkage is particularly noticeable in organizations that have a reasonable level of formal training and development, and where market conditions (such as hygiene standards) impose certain specific training and development activities. This was the case in the two meat-processing firms in our study.

Where training policies exist, they are designed to provide the enterprise with the *minimum* requirements needed to retain a productive workforce, irrespective of the degree of formality. This is due to the need to minimize training expenditures and the competitive pressure to focus on the shorter term where there is less perceived need for more advanced skills. To a considerable extent, the lack of a formal training policy derives from the nature of production of the small firms in the sectors studied, where work processes use simple mature technologies which require little or no advanced skills. Most often the educational requirement is basic primary education. No pre-existing skills are required, and there is a tendency in the small firms studied to view external training as an avoidable operation cost. This lower valuation of training and skills is also a consequence of the less stable workforce due to the high level of dependence on seasonal and temporary workers. However, the introduction of technology may increase the need for more advanced and formalized training. For example, in Tebe Mills a plan to introduce new machinery will require the firm to invest more in training.

Some firms under-invest because they believe that a large investment in training puts them at greater risk of having their employees poached by other enterprises who seek workers with higher levels of skills. But others invest in training and link incentives to use that training most effectively with their longer-term retention strategy. At Twikki Meat recruits who successfully complete on-the-job training enjoy an increase in their salaries to motivate and retain them.

Less investment in formal training in the firms studied may also be due to the fact that the shared community background of workers and a less formal atmosphere are conducive to the transfer of skills between workers, so the needed skills can be more easily acquired on the job. On-the-job training is carried out through induction, assigning new employees to work alongside more experienced workers, and learning by doing. On-the-job training may involve areas beyond production, such as safety and health and environmental management. In some cases outside specialists are occasionally brought in to give lectures, generally on new developments in the industry and on safety issues.

Although small firms display varying approaches to the issue of training, in general they do recognize the importance of ensuring that workers have the minimum requisite skills and an understanding of the importance of effectiveness and productivity. Several small firms studied are taking the issue of productivity very seriously, particularly those that face intense competition, whether locally or externally. In the Philippines, Kenya and Nepal, where firms face external competition, productivity improvement training is a common practice among firms. At Shikhar Maida and Taja Bakery, management initiated training programmes on 5S (productivity and clean production, see page 34) in the 1990s (see box 4). Similar training schemes have been introduced at Sumsuman Foods and Masapat Farms, including training on more complex productivity improvement schemes, good housekeeping programmes, HACCP, job enrichment, job rotation and good management practices (GMP), and standard operating procedures. Firms in Kenya and the Philippines also conduct team-building seminars.

In some cases, training is required because of the requirement for entry into foreign markets, especially in the United States. Masapat Farms and Twikki Meat are in the process of entering the international meat market, which has strict processing standards, so their training programmes are highly formalized and taken very seriously. In such cases, off-the-job training is

Box 4    The link between training and retention strategies: The case of small enterprises in Nepal

Nepal provides a good example of the effect of a country developing training, recruiting and retention policies in isolation rather than as an integrated approach. It also demonstrates the value of collective bargaining concerning skills development, and how sometimes a sector-wide approach is needed.

Nepalese enterprises such as Suddha Vanaspati and Mitho Chau Chau Foods provide some training on an ad hoc basis to orient new workers. Nonetheless, managers generally complain of a dearth of skilled workers yet make no systematic effort to provide training. The only training programmes that exist are provided by third parties on an occasional basis, such as the participation of workers at Shikhar Maida and Taja Bakery in productivity improvement training programmes such as 5s and Kaisan provided by the National Productivity and Economic Development Center (NPEDC).

Why don't these enterprises do more to raise the skills level of their workers, despite the great need they have identified? The employers interviewed felt that it is the responsibility of the government to provide training across an entire sector because of the high risk of poaching which discourages any single firm from investing in skills development. Why invest scarce resources in training the competition's workforce? In addition, employers feel that the newly trained workers will demand higher wages and more workplace amenities, which will further increase the cost of training.

The sector-wide provision of basic skills through a sector-specific training centre would counter to some extent the fear of poaching. Furthermore, firms can reduce the likelihood of poaching by developing a synergy between their policy for skills development and policies for recruiting and retaining more productive workers. And enterprises can reach agreements with the workers' representatives about the appropriate rate of wage and amenity increases linked to higher skills levels. These simple steps could do a lot to shift employers' attitudes towards investing in skills development, to everyone's benefit.

common. For instance, Twikki Meat has sent more than 20 workers to off-site training provided industry-wide.

Supervisors generally decide who requires training, based primarily on their personal knowledge of each worker they supervise. Where skills requirements are low, promotion to the supervisory grade in the firms studied tends to be based on length of service, experience and good conduct rather than on formal education and training. However, many small firms in the food sub-sector have a relatively high level of professional managers despite the lack of formal training for the general workforce. At Ugali Tamu, training is given in accounting, marketing, computing and other management development programmes, whereas on-the-job training for general workers is brief and more like induction, and stresses product knowledge and how to handle customer issues.

Some small firms also provide training in general knowledge to help workers to recognize simple instructions on how to do their work effectively. In enterprises where such training is conducted, it is given either as general training or for a specific cadre of workers. Thus at Mchuzi Safi the firm believes that knowledgeable sales people in particular are the key to company success and focuses job training on equipping its sales staff with the skills, knowledge and attitudes needed to be most effective.

Small firms may also provide training to help workers develop broader skills. Taja Bakery encourages its mainly female workforce to participate in vocational training such as knitting, sewing and painting, as a service to workers to equip them with skills which they can use for their own personal benefit. Workers also have the opportunity of joining weekly literacy classes inside or outside the company. Such training has the potential added benefit of improving the competence of a largely illiterate workforce in performing its tasks, but the main focus is on improving workers' ability to generate additional income.

## Wages and compensation policies

The firms interviewed were, on the one hand, reluctant to divulge specific details about the wages and benefits they paid their employees. On the other hand, many felt that they treated their workers quite well and were proud of their policies more generally.

In small firms, as in many enterprises, the most important element of a company human resources management policy is the compensation package. For workers in general, wage compensation is the most significant reward for work. This is even more so in small enterprises such as the ones studied here, because workers typically come from rural areas where they have received only a minimal education. In many cases, the workers were engaged in formal sector employment for the first time and considered themselves very lucky to have escaped the large pool of unemployed people in the community. Owners of small firms also believed that they were helping the workers to have a meaningful life in the community by providing jobs in the formal economy. This sense of moral obligation critically influenced their wage policies, although employers were also constrained by market competition and the economic environment in which they operate.

As in most areas of the human resources policy, both formal and informal processes characterize the wage policy in the firms studied. Generally, entrepreneurs take the minimum wage as either the baseline or the reference point for their wage policies. Other than this general adoption of the minimum wage, there is no uniformity in the scope for applying each wage policy, even among firms within the same country. The wide variety of policies reflects the variation between firms concerning economic performance and overall approach to the employment relationship. However, despite the variations in the wage polices, they all have in common a strong concern to contain the wage bill, since the food sub-sectors in the countries included in the study have relatively low profit margins.

Generally the prevailing minimum wage in the country, region or industry is applied as the going wage for the lowest-paid core workers, and serves as the floor upon which wages for higher categories of workers are based. On the other hand, practice in the small firms studied concerning the wages for non-core categories of workers, such as various types of contingent workers, varied more. For instance, a comparison of practices in two firms in the Philippines showed that one paid core workers P210–P240 per day compared to the statutory minimum wage of P200 for the region in 2003, but paid seasonal workers only P160 per day; in contrast, core and casual workers in the other firm both received the minimum wage prevailing for the province. Mitho Chau Chau in Nepal pays the minimum wage to contingent workers, whether temporary, casual or daily-rated workers.

In addition to the basic wage, most of the enterprises studied also stated that they comply with other legal provisions concerning compensation, such as additional compensation for overtime and work during public holidays. For instance, in Botswana the small enterprises studied pay workers the required hourly overtime rate of 150 per cent, and 200 per cent for work on rest days and public holidays.

Wages are generally adjusted for cost-of-living increases, in accordance with legislation, although some firms are reluctant to fully commit themselves to this practice, or may limit it to certain categories of workers. Tebe Mills reviews wage levels every two years, in compliance with the minimum wage legislation; but states in its handbook that the enterprise does not bind itself to revise its salary scales, notwithstanding any increase in the cost of living, or any national cost-of-living increase awarded to employees generally. Suddha Vanaspati complies with the minimum wage requirements, but it grants annual wage increases of 5 per cent exclusively to permanent workers.

In addition to considerations of changes in the cost of living, some firms also link pay increases to performance. For example, Tebe Mills increases wages based on annual performance evaluation, in the range of 6 to 12 per cent. Twikki Meat also takes performance into consideration, but its handbook does not commit to particular targets.

The food sub-sector requires relatively low skills, so most compensation policies did not differentiate between workers based on skill levels. However, some firms, such as Maziwa, paid the minimum wage to entry-level workers and paid more to experienced workers with more skills. And one firm was in the process of changing its wage policy to reflect differences in skills and experience, in response to complaints from more senior employees.

In addition to wages, small firms generally paid bonuses not linked to performance. Some are mandated by law, such as payment of a 13th month of wages required by law in the Philippines. Others are discretionary and are linked to company profits for the year. For example, Twikki Meat pays general bonuses, which range from 5 to 10 per cent of a worker's salary and may be paid at the end of the financial year, depending on the company's profitability, with a gratuity paid every five years. Another common practice is to give a festival allowance or gift to workers on religious holidays, such as the Desai festival in Nepal. Additionally, there is the almost universal practice among the firms studied to provide products to workers, either free or at concessionary rates. Entrepreneurs make such gestures partly out of a sense of obligation to their workers, and partly as a means of strengthening the bond of loyalty and commitment to the enterprise, albeit sometimes with the express intent of dissuading workers from joining unions.

Some firms also encourage workers to engage in outside activities to supplement their income. For instance, Masapat Farms in the Philippines has established cooperatives to help workers to earn extra money.

## Benefits and other conditions of work

The small firms studied broadly comply with the applicable laws concerning benefits and other conditions of employment; however, firms typically apply the general conditions of employment selectively. While most small firms comply with laws regulating the payment of overtime and the treatment of public holidays, compliance with provisions concerning such issues as leave and medical benefits is more varied.

There is no trend in provision of benefits in the small firms studied, only a continuum. Approaches range from not meeting most basic legal requirements to providing benefits well beyond what is required by law. Mchuzi Safi in Kenya does not provide medical coverage for workers, and is currently involved in a legal dispute on this issue; while Maziwa and Ugali Tamu each provide medical services through a health unit located within the organization, dependants were not entitled to these benefits. In Suddha Vanaspati in Nepal medical check-ups are paid for by the firm, but there is no established policy on medical services to the workers or their dependants. On the other hand, Shikhar Maida provides medical benefits up to a maximum of 25 per cent of salary, while Taja Bakery provides first aid for workers on the company premises, refers major injuries to the hospital at the company's expense and is considering the introduction of a health insurance scheme.

Several of the firms provide accident or medical insurance, or other social security benefits for workers. At Suddha Vanaspati, Taja Bakery and Tebe

Mills, for example, medical insurance or full payment of medical expenses is provided to workers. Suddha Vanaspati also provides general accident insurance for workers. Sumsuman Foods, Dagatyaman and Masapat Farms provide maternity leave, retirement, health care and accident insurance schemes. In both Suddha Vanaspati and Shikhar Maida , female workers are entitled to maternity leave with pay for one month, as required by law.

As in the case of minimum wage requirements, distinctions are often made between core and non-core workers. For example, the three Filipino firms studied limited statutory benefits to core workers, as permitted by law.

While firms generally limited paid leave to the minimum required by law, some firms, such as Mchuzi Safi, give more leave days on the basis of seniority. Most firms limit leave to certain categories of workers; Twikki Meat, for example, limits the categories of staff who qualify for annual leave, sick leave, compassionate leave, maternity leave, study leave and unpaid leave.

It may seem less than impressive for enterprises to meet the minimum legal obligations, and even then only selectively. However, it must be borne in mind that such legal requirements, although essential to protect the welfare of workers, are often constructed in a manner that does not take into consideration the financial burdens they place on smaller firms. For instance, the per capita cost to a small employer of providing on-site medical service is much greater for an enterprise with 50 workers than one with 1000 workers.

Furthermore, despite the numerous areas where these small enterprises fall short of their legal obligations, it appears that they all have an explicit policy to provide as many benefits as possible, devising means for balancing the entitlements of workers with the needs of the enterprise. For example, at Maziwa workers are entitled to 21 days annual leave, but the taking of leave is staggered so as to facilitate continuous production.

In addition, several firms studied provide a range of benefits which are not required by law. At Shikhar Maida core workers are entitled to an education allowance for up to two children and may receive an advance of two years' salary to purchase land. Taja Bakery provides benefits such as accommodation in a company dormitory for night-shift workers and a meal for workers on each shift, to improve the work environment and facilitate workers' safety and comfort.

Some analysts, such as Atkinson and Storey (1994) have argued that employment conditions are poor in SMEs compared to larger companies because of the greater financial constraints and market pressures they face. While this perception is generally justified, most of the firms in this study do not entirely fit the description. Many were within the average for the sector, and some were even competitive with the average wage for the higher-paid manufacturing sector (see box 5). For those firms which fell below the average, the driving force was more likely a lack of financial resources rather

Box 5     Summary of wages and benefits policies in the small enterprises
          studied

**Botswana**
*Tebe Mills*
Workers are paid the minimum wage plus an individual performance bonus. The wage scales are being revised to take into account experience and skills. A premium is paid for overtime. Management has also established a burial society (insurance to cover funeral costs) in response to the HIV/AIDS pandemic.

*Twikki Meat*
Workers' wages range from P500 (the statutory minimum) to P4,500, with performance bonuses of 5-10 per cent of salary tied to the profits of the company. Gratuity is paid every five years. Workers receive discounts on products; breakfast and lunch is provided; washing facilities are provided. Workers are also covered by general accident and health insurance; and the management plans to provide life insurance and establish a burial society.

**Kenya**
*Maziwa*
Workers are paid approximately 60 per cent above the statutory minimum.

*Mchuzi Safi*
Workers are paid more than twice the statutory minimum for the region; they are also provided with lunch and receive a Christmas gift.

*Ugali Tamu*
Workers are paid approximately 10 per cent above the statutory minimum for the region.

**Nepal**
*Mitho Chau Chau Foods*
Permanent workers are paid all statutory wages and benefits, including participation in the provident fund, paid public holidays, overtime premium, holiday bonuses and paid leave. But the vast majority of workers are classified as temporary workers and are paid only the minimum wage, although they are entitled to paid public holidays. Contract workers are paid the statutory piece rate with no entitlements.

*Shikhar Maida*
Unskilled workers are paid Rs2,100-3,300 (the statutory minimum is Rs.2,100) up to Rs4,400 for highly skilled workers. Workers also receive statutory allowances for dress, shoes and a raincoat, housing, medical care, and transport. Workers also are entitled to an advance on their salary equivalent to up to 2 years' salary to buy land; and an advance of 6-12 months of salary for other needs. They are entitled to an education allowance for up to two children.

*Suddha Vanaspati*
Workers are paid the statutory minimum, with only irregular bonuses and a limited night-time premium below the statutory requirements.

*/cont'd.*

Box 5    Summary of wages and benefits policies in the small enterprises
         studied *(cont'd)*

*Taja Bakery*
The wage varies from the statutory minimum (Rs1,800) for new employees up to
Rs3,500 for more experienced workers and workers in comparatively technical jobs.
Workers are also provided with: accommodation for night-shift workers; overtime
allowance required by law, a hot meal, festival leave totalling 10 days, a festival
allowance equal to one month's salary, a performance-based bonus (paid in cash and
gifts); a monthly attendance-rate bonus; and a dress allowance. The company plans
to introduce health insurance and savings accounts for workers.

**Philippines**
*Dagatyaman Seafood*
The company has six salary grades, with six steps per grade. Regular daily wages
range from P210 to P240 per day, but contractual workers and seasonal workers
receive only P160 per day. The statutory minimum is P200. The company justifies this
by the fact that most of the seasonal workers are relatives of regular employees, and
it seeks to spread the casual employment over more workers.

Permanent employees also receive the statutory 13th month of pay, and mid-year and
end-of-year bonuses and groceries at Christmas.

Permanent workers receive all statutory benefits: social security, medical insurance,
vacation leave, five paid sick days per year, two months paid maternity leave. In
addition, permanent workers may take out life insurance, with the employer paying 75
per cent of the premium.

*Masapat Farms*
Regular workers are paid P275 per day (statutory minimum is P225) with overtime and
premium pay for night work and holidays. In addition, they receive a 13th month of
salary, a Christmas gift, and a discount of 25 per cent on products; they are covered
by a retirement plan, health care plan, and general accident insurance, and are entitled
to five days sick leave and five days vacation leave per annum.

Workers still on probation receive only the minimum wage and are covered by accident
insurance.

*Sumsuman Foods*
All employees receive: regionally set minimum wage, performance-based premium and
productivity bonuses tied to net earnings, statutory overtime premium, and night-shift
premium.

than a failure to appreciate the importance of paying workers well. The limited
financial resources of many small enterprises constrain their ability to provide
higher wages and benefits for the entire workforce, forcing them to prioritize
either through restricting benefits or restricting who benefits. The cases also

show, though, that workers in organized firms undoubtedly enjoy higher wages and benefits than those in comparable unorganized firms.

## The determination of wages and conditions

Criticisms of employment conditions in SMEs, in particular lower wages and more limited benefits, focus on the lack of worker representation or voice in the process which could help workers to leverage their negotiating power. Although it is true that in general more formal worker participation in the setting of wages and benefits tends to lead to better outcomes for workers, the complex web of relations within a small firm, the stronger influence of environmental and communal factors, the structure of financing and concentration of risk, and the strong presence of the entrepreneur's personality and preferences complicates the story.

Of the enterprises studied, there was rarely a complete absence of consultation with workers on wages and conditions of work. In some cases, national law requires consultation. Under the labour code in the Philippines, workers have the right to participate in policy and decisions on employment conditions regardless of whether they are organized, although this right is not always respected in practice in small firms and obviously is more easily ignored in the absence of a union. Even when no legal obligation exists, some firms studied were open to listening to workers' views. For example, Twikki Meat is unorganized, and management alone determines wages and conditions of service; yet workers can influence these decisions through their suggestions and complaints, which are routed through their supervisors who often attend meetings with management. If the supervisors do not appear to achieve results, workers can make their suggestions directly to management. Nonetheless, unlike organized enterprises, the workers at Twikki Meat have no formal means of collectively gathering and sharing information and expressing their needs and concerns; and they lack the means to pursue their requests through organized action.

But the existence of workers' representatives is not in itself a guarantee that workers will have an effective voice, because management's attitude towards unions is an equally important consideration. Fewer than half of the firms studied accepted to enter into negotiations with workers' representatives. For instance, Suddha Vanaspati has workers' representatives at the enterprise level, but management rarely sits down with the representatives in formal negotiations on wages and conditions. Managers explained that this was due partly to poor financial conditions, and partly because of hostility towards the union. Similarly, at Mchuzi Safi management used to set wages by first considering the statutory minimum wage provisions for each category of staff, and then added a top-up of 5-8 per cent per year, depending on business performance. However, when the enterprise became organized, management decided to strictly adhere to the provisions of the national law governing collective bargaining; as a result, the wages of the unionized staff have remained constant since 2002 as they await the outcome of an economic trade dispute pending at the industrial court.

The attitude of management to unions is not the only factor influencing structure and issues for negotiations in enterprises with workers' representatives; other factors include the level of collective bargaining and the level of maturity of the bargaining relationship. Shikhar Maida has workers' representatives at the enterprise level and management negotiates with them. From 1982 to around 2000 the negotiation process was formal. But as the level of trust and cooperation between union officials and management matured, negotiations started to take on a less formal structure and to occur more frequently over a broader range of issues.

Mitho Chau Chau Foods has workers' representatives affiliated with two confederations which form a joint committee to negotiate with management. Negotiations address a broad range of issues, such as making more workers permanent, leave, insurance coverage, childcare, and office facilities for the union.

At Maziwa, Mchuzi Safi and Ugali Tamu in Kenya, bargaining occurs at the sector level. The workers' representatives at the enterprise level are not necessarily involved in negotiations, but the workers are covered by the sectoral agreement. They are able to participate indirectly in the process through their representatives' participation in the unions and confederation.

When management sets wages and conditions of services unilaterally, it generally pays attention to the legal minimum wage, and changes in the basic pay are made according to the official minimum wage review requirements. The legal minimum wage is the outcome of a tripartite consultation process at the national or regional level in the four countries included in the study. Hence, unions played an important role in wage determination in all of the enterprises studied, even if only indirectly through setting baselines.

Some unorganized enterprises paid workers above the minimum required by law. At Ugali Tamu, although there is no collective bargaining relationship, the enterprise paid all workers at least the minimum wage, and paid non-management staff an average monthly wage 10.7 per cent above the minimum wage. Management at Maziwa stated that it set a target of annual percentage increase ranging from 6 to 8 per cent, which is above the rate of increase required by law, specifically because workers were not involved in wage-fixing processes and hence management felt that it had a greater duty to protect the workers' interests.

This paternalistic attitude towards unorganized workers was common. In the unorganized enterprises studied, management generally considered that their compensation policies were superior to whatever the union might be able to get for the workers. For example, at Masapat Farms management believes that the unilateral management decision to establish cooperatives was very important to the welfare of the workers and to improve their quality of life; and that such gestures on the part of management were sufficient to meet the needs of workers, making a union unnecessary.

Although organization of workers and formal negotiation are not essential, a complete absence of consultation with workers on wages and benefits is a missed opportunity to build stronger labour–management cooperation.

## Performance appraisal and the reward system

The small firms studied generally appreciated the link between good performance and reward to motivate workers, and some have introduced a performance appraisal system for this purpose.

Managers typically conducted informal appraisals where the parameters used included employee performance, discipline, punctuality, attendance and honesty. The outcome was used to make decisions on bonuses, discipline, promotion and employee discharge.

When a system is not based on any clearly defined procedure, and involves only managers, it tends to create low motivation and a poor relationship between management and the workers. In contrast, the few firms which have made their appraisal systems more formal, transparent and inclusive have gained a lot from linking performance and reward. For instance, Tebe Mills has introduced a three-stage performance appraisal process: first the workers appraise themselves; then the workers are appraised by their supervisors; lastly, the worker and supervisor meet to discuss and agree on the appraisal. The agreed outcome forms the basis of the worker's performance-linked compensation, and has helped to improve labour–management cooperation and ultimately productivity and competitiveness.

Of course, tying rewards to individual performance rather than group performance risks eroding worker solidarity and team effort, which can work against productivity improvement. To overcome this problem, some firms link bonuses to firm profitability rather than individual performance, with the same amount or percentage paid across the board. Others, such as Tebe Mills, pay bonuses or give prizes privately to the worker concerned, to avoid any discord among the workforce; or, like Sumsuman Foods, provide a combination of individual and group incentives.

## Disciplinary and grievance procedures

Several of the enterprises studied had formal grievance and discipline procedures, as well as dispute resolution mechanisms. For instance, the three firms in the Philippines all had elaborate and formal disciplinary procedures, which were written either in specific disciplinary codes or in the employee handbook. However, the majority of firms stressed the importance of a flexible approach, to allow more leeway in dealing with problems on the part of either the workers or management.

In the area of discipline, management in most firms was concerned about the impact of perceived lapses in discipline and decreased productivity. However, the aims of discipline were sometimes more broadly defined. For instance, according to management at Sumsuman Foods, the whole vision and philosophy of the enterprise are related to the disciplinary rules. And at Masapat Farms disciplinary offences include a range of behaviours from productivity performance to personal conduct outside of working hours: in addition to absenteeism and other typical disciplinary issues, management also includes in the list of offences violation of any 5S rules such as erratic filing of documents or not wearing gloves or masks while in contact with meat; as well as taking liquor inside or outside company premises at any time.

In most cases, management was responsible for enforcing discipline. But some enterprises relied in the first instance on peer pressure from co-workers. The employee handbook at Twikki Meat specifies a disciplinary procedure, but authorizes and encourages workers to discuss discipline among themselves, including problems related to drunkenness, tardiness or absenteeism. If a worker does not change, the co-workers are instructed to report the matter to the supervisor, who is authorized to take the initial disciplinary measures set out in the handbook. Likewise, at Tebe Mills the very broad nature of consultation and information dissemination practices among and between staff has resulted in the empowerment of workers to replace absent members of the production team, and to recommend dismissal for team members who are persistently absent.

However, other firms make efforts not to encourage too much mutual policing among workers, or confrontation between workers which may harm team work. For instance, at Dagatyaman sole responsibility for discipline rests with the production supervisor; and in the case of absenteeism and tardiness, confrontation is avoided altogether with a computerized fingerprint time-keeping system which is linked to the payroll system and which automatically deducts pay for absences and tardiness, without the need for management to take corrective action.

Issues cited for disciplinary measures were very similar across most enterprises, and included: tardiness, drunkenness, disobeying supervisors, bribery, theft, fraud, embezzlement and so on, but by far the most cited disciplinary problem was absenteeism. In some cases, it is indeed a national problem rooted in customs and festivals, and in gender biases. For instance, in Nepal women workers are very commonly absent during the period before festivals because they are expected to do most of the work entailed in the celebrations. To counter this problem, Taja Bakery has developed a programme to sensitize the families of their female employees, offering them tours of the plant and explaining the important role the women workers play in the production process and how vital their presence is, even during pre-festival periods. In another example, absenteeism in small firms in Botswana is more common among men, and has to do with drunkenness, especially following payment of wages.

Most firms had no formal procedure for dealing with infractions, but the informal process generally included giving the worker the chance to be heard. However, Sumsuman Foods has implemented a more formal procedure to ensure the right to defend oneself against allegations that could result in disciplinary action. A meeting is held among all parties concerned and their witnesses, the human resources manager and management. Notice is given to inform the worker of the allegation, and a formal investigation is conducted. The employee is given the opportunity to defend himself or herself against the accusation before management decides on the penalty to be imposed if the person is found liable.

Penalties imposed generally include a warning for a first offence; where there is no improvement, the worker is suspended; and as a last resort, his or her employment is terminated. Immediate dismissal is usually limited to grave offences such as endangering the lives of other workers. However, at Ugali Tamu any physical confrontation, smoking or drinking on the job are considered serious enough to warrant immediate dismissal. And in addressing tardiness and absenteeism, Sumsuman Foods recently switched from suspension without pay (which reportedly did not serve as an effective deterrent) to "decision-making leave", whereby the person sanctioned is put on leave without pay for a day to think about whether he or she wants to continue working for the company, and is required to write a promissory letter not to commit the same offence again or the next infraction may lead to dismissal.

Some enterprises made positive efforts to address the cause of the most common disciplinary problems. For example, Tebe Mills instituted a practice of paying wages at the start of the weekend, to allow workers to enjoy their wages while avoiding absenteeism problems. In several firms, incentives are offered for attendance at work or for good behaviour generally: Taja Bakery,

> **Box 6      A typical grievance procedure: Twikki Meat**
>
> As with the majority of small firms surveyed, there is no union at Twikki Meat. Grievances are therefore only dealt with at the individual level. An employee who has a grievance arising out of conditions of employment or any other problem other than a matter concerning disciplinary action, must raise the grievance with his immediate supervisor within 14 days of his becoming aware of such problem. The supervisor should settle the grievance within seven working days, failing which the employee may raise the grievance with his section manager. If the section manager is not able to settle the grievance to the satisfaction of the employee within another seven days, the employee may then raise his grievance in writing with the Managing Director whose decision is final and has to be conveyed to the employee within 30 calendar days.

for example, offers Rs100 per month as an incentive for avoiding absences. And at Sumsuman Foods workers are encouraged to join in a morning prayer before the start of work three times a week, as part of an overall approach to promoting discipline.

Concerning grievances, the small firms studied usually had a system that on the one hand aimed to address issues in a less formal manner, but on the other hand operated through the various hierarchies of managers and supervisors all the way to the owner-manager (see box 6). Generally, any dispute resolution mechanisms that existed did not involve workers or their representatives, often with harmful consequences for labour–management cooperation. In Mchuzi Safi where there is no formal consultative machinery despite the existence of a trade union, a substantial number of trade disputes have been brought to the labour court during the past four years, and the high level of worker dissatisfaction has led to acrimonious relations between management and workers, seriously undermining productivity. However, some firms did engage workers in grievance resolutions on an informal basis. For instance, at Taja Bakery the owner-manager attends the consultative meetings at the end of every month, and uses the meeting to go through staff grievances concerning wages and other work-related issues.

Most disputes related to issues such as wrongful dismissal, wages, and leave. A key grievance in unionized enterprises was the belief that management was not transparent enough.

## Occupational safety and health

Workers and managers interviewed both agreed that occupational safety and health (OSH) directly contribute to good performance, enterprise productivity and competitiveness. Consistent with this view the small firms incorporated aspects of the national safety and health statutes into their human resources practices pertaining to, inter alia, the work environment, a clean workplace, work clothes, safe behaviour, injuries at work, and safety awareness.

Many of the firms were selective in deciding which elements of statutory OSH requirements they enforced in the workplace, mainly owing to cost considerations. Nonetheless, safety and health issues are seen by small firms as critical to the prevention of accidents and occupational illness and disease. Thus these firms take seriously issues such as the wearing of masks, uniform or work clothes, and fire and sickness prevention. Additionally, most small firms link their OSH practices to their welfare programme for workers. Owing to the nature of the food sector, the safety and health regime is also directly linked to the productivity and quality programmes.

The degree of consultation with workers on OSH issues varied substantially among the firms studied. Many have adopted an informal bipartite approach to addressing the issue of safety and health, in which consultations and meetings are regularly held between managers and workers. At Tebe Mills, for instance, issues concerning safety and health are regularly discussed at meetings between the owner, the supervisors and the workers. In contrast, firms such as Ugali Tamu, Mchuzi Safi and Taja Bakery do not have any consultative machinery, and OSH practices are entirely the responsibility of management. In some cases, formal institutional structures for OSH, such as a safety committee for bipartite consultation, do not exist in the firms studied even when consultation committees traditionally exist for other purposes. In Nepal, for example, where it is both customary and a legal obligation to set up a safety committee, Shikhar Maida stated that it was planning to set one up but had not done so yet.

There are notable differences in the scope of the safety and health regimes in small firms. In some firms, such as Taja Bakery, Shikhar Maida, Tebe Mills, Mchuzi Safi and Maziwa, the safety regimes are rarely more than adherence to the basic standards, including first aid, provision of work clothes or uniforms, apparel such as masks, and posters in workplaces. Other firms went beyond this minimum, in part because they viewed the safety and health regimes as part of the their productivity and welfare schemes. For example, at Taja Bakery workers on the night shift are provided with sleeping facilities after work rather than risk walking home alone, in an effort to support the worker but also to contribute to productivity, since workers can better concentrate when they are not anxious about getting home safely.

Some firms provided on-site access to medical care. Maziwa has a medical unit on the company premises. In contrast, Mchuzi Safi provides no medical assistance on site to injured workers, which was one of the issues raised in a dispute brought to the industrial court. Often, in case of accident the doctor who treats the employee also assesses the level of injury for the purpose of determining compensation, as for example at Tebe Mills.

All the enterprises studied provide some degree of periodic or regular training on safety and health. In enterprises such as Sumsuman Foods, safety training and awareness in such areas as job safety, accidents, fire fighting and the use of fire extinguishers are part of an in-house training video programme offered three times a week. This is supplemented by quarterly guest presentations on a variety of performance-enhancing issues.

HIV/AIDS is a health topic of particular concern for the African enterprises studied. At Tebe Mills, occasional lectures are given on HIV/AIDS. Management at Twikki Meat organizes lectures and discussion on HIV/AIDS issues, distributes condoms and makes them available in company toilets. Community nurses and other officials of organizations engaged in HIV/AIDS education and prevention activities provide preventive education.

The adoption of basic OSH standards in small firms in the food sector has also been buttressed in general by the requirements of the food industry, which obliges firms to adhere to certain basic minimum industry-specific standards on quality and health and safety. Several enterprises studied subscribe to various certification programmes such as Hazard Analysis Critical Control Point (HACCP), Good Manufacturing Practices (GMP), and International Standardization Organization (ISO) Certification. Firms seeking to export processed foods are required to pay particular attention to OSH issues. Dagatyaman and Ugali Tamu, which already export, and Twikki Meat and Masapat Farms, both of which are planning to enter the export market, all stressed the critical role of hygiene, health and safety. To achieve a highly hygienic work environment, these firms provide meals to keep workers from going outside the factory premises in order to avoid contamination; and workers are medically examined before they are employed and annually thereafter to ensure that they are free of any communicable disease. Inspections are usually unscheduled to ensure that the factory is kept clean at all times. Consequently, these firms have an extensive training programme on OSH, compared with other types of training provided. For instance, in 2003 alone Masapat Farms provided training on food safety for 80 per cent of its workers, as part of its participation in various certification programmes.

Despite the relatively casual approach to OSH practices and the limited scope of safety and health issues, the small firms studied appear to have attained a reasonable level of safety and health, and a very low rate of industrial accidents or occupational diseases was reported. For example, in the 10 years Twikki Meat has been in operation there has been only one major accident, which is exceptional for the meat-processing industry. Workers at Twikki Meat attribute the high safety record to the rigorous maintenance of production machines – workers ensure that any faults are promptly reported and management ensures that they are quickly repaired. It must be added, though, that these firms generally do not keep records of their safety and health issues, due in part to the informality of the safety and health regimes in most small firms. Lax enforcement of OSH regulations through inspections encourages firms to continue with the informal approach. Although informality has some advantages, it can act as a barrier to upgrading the OSH policies and procedures in a firm.

## The role of respect for the right to organize in promoting labour–management cooperation

Freedom of association is a fundamental right for both workers and employers. For workers, active participation – in contrast with being the passive recipient of another's will – affirms and reinforces one's dignity. This is the inherent limitation of any paternalistic management or governing strategy: however much it seeks to be benevolent, it does not affirm human dignity. This is why a voice in society and in the workplace has no substitute. Furthermore, because freedom of association is a human right, respect for this right is increasingly demanded by buyers and consumers. Therefore, failure to respect the right of association may cost an enterprise valuable business.

Freedom of association is important for employers, including small enterprises. Many issues are shared by all employers in a sector, or across an economy. Employers' and workers' organizations can find creative solutions to problems, such as shared resources to reduce the cost of training, technology improvements, and so on. Employers' organizations can more effectively make their concerns known to workers' organizations and the government. For instance, if the competitive position of exporting firms is being harmed by the government's exchange rate policy, an employers' organization can lobby the government to change its policy much more effectively than the uncoordinated efforts of individual small producers.

Unions can play an important role in facilitating the flow of information and promoting labour–management cooperation by:

- providing information about what occurs on the shop floor, by encouraging workers to express their views and provide suggestions, and by acting as a messenger for workers who are afraid to appear to be criticizing their supervisors. By acting as a funnel for information, unions can also provide a sense of perspective, whether a problem is recurring or unique to one production unit;

- improving morale by giving workers a sense that their views count, and that they are not helpless to do anything about problems;

- pressuring management to be more efficient, mainly through closing off the low-price route to competition. Firms must compete on other dimensions to survive, such as quality, innovativeness, delivery rates, and so on;

- seeking to minimize workers' exposure to the risk of job loss by negotiating rules for fairness in dismissal. This curbs the excessive behaviour of some managers which can poison the working relationship for everyone;

- providing a voice at work and in democratic societies. They provide a significant but often overlooked perspective on a range of issues in the workplace, community and society. This is important not only for the valuable information unions contribute, but also for the validity of decisions made in the workplace and society. A fundamental concept underlying democracy is that voice lends legitimacy and helps to build support for decisions taken;

- helping to reduce inequality in society through collective bargaining which tends to raise the wages of less-skilled workers. Higher rates of union density are associated with less extremes of wealth (fewer super-rich and fewer desperately poor people). Unions increase industrial democracy through conditioning management to share decision-making with workers;

- increasing productivity of firms, in large part through motivating them to be more efficient because they do not have the option of competing on price alone. They also help increase productivity because better-paid workers tend to be more motivated. And employers tend to invest more in higher-paid workers with more job security because they are more likely to remain with the firm, so that the employer's yield on the investment lasts for a longer period of time; and

- addressing sensitive issues among members such as substance abuse and HIV/AIDS, which can have a profound impact on the lives of workers, the work environment and productivity. These issues are often too sensitive to be addressed directly by management, but management can support union efforts to help their members (time off work, help with resources, and so on).

This is aggregate data on union potential which is often seen in economic research (Freeman and Medoff, 1984). What any particular union does depends on the context in which it exists. Unions do not exist in a vacuum; they respond to the environment created by management (in firms with controlling management strategies) or created with management (in firms with participatory management strategies).

## Worker organization in the firms studied

Managers may choose to communicate with workers individually or collectively, and tend to do both. Even in very small firms it is time-consuming and inefficient to communicate with workers on a one-on-one basis for issues that concern all workers, such as explaining safety measures or negotiating work schedules. Furthermore, there is not much advantage to be gained from individual discussions and negotiations on issues such as wages and benefits, since differential treatment will quickly be made known among the workers and can cause resentment. Therefore, the enterprises studied generally interacted with the workers as a group when addressing issues of concern to all of them.

Workers, in turn, may choose to organize themselves formally in a union. Of the twelve enterprises studied, five have had trade unions for at least some period, and four were presently active. An ILO study on SMEs found that in general workers in small enterprises, particularly in developing countries, tend not to join trade unions (ILO, 1995). This is, of course, their right, if freely exercised.

There are many possible explanations why workers in small enterprises often choose not to organize to express their interests and concerns more effectively. On the one hand, it may be that such workers do not feel the need to organize formally – the proximity of workers and managers and direct lines of communication may make a more formal representative structure unnecessary or perhaps even awkward. Flatter hierarchies also increase the likelihood of greater involvement of workers in operational decision-making, more interaction and consultation between managers and workers, and better communication and receptivity to new ideas. These aspects may give workers a greater voice in the workplace compared to larger enterprises, despite the absence of a union structure. It may also be that in a particular country, historically unions have not existed in privately owned enterprises, which makes workers less inclined to organize.

The enterprises studied reveal a range of worker perceptions about unions, many of which were consistent with this view. In the case of Tebe Mills in Botswana, national union representatives approached the workers about organizing the workplace. The workers declined the offer of assistance for a variety of reasons. They considered that existing channels of communication were adequate, relations were relatively harmonious, and they were able to voice concerns and grievances adequately in periodic meetings organized along operational functions. Therefore, they felt that the union membership dues they would pay would not bring much in the way of additional benefits.

The desire of workers not to organize was in one case due to the previous history of the company. Dagatyaman evolved out of the remains of a firm which went under partly because of the financial losses caused by a prolonged union strike. The entrepreneur-owner of the new firm, who had been an employee of the old one, hired many of his fellow employees to work at the new enterprise. Workers expressed gratitude for the new jobs, felt they had a good relationship with the owner, and chose not to organize based on their previous experience.

Some workers were reluctant to organize or participate in a union out of concern that union activity at the sector level could change the character of relations in the workplace. At Mchuzi Safi in Kenya, 40 per cent of eligible workers were unionized by the bakery union, but the acrimonious labour relations in the industry as a whole appeared to have dampened the interest of both workers and management to fully embrace union activity. Management and the majority of workers shared the view that the behaviour of the union in the sector was confrontational.

On the other hand, workers may want to organize but may not feel at liberty to do so, given the entrepreneur's strong, and strongly expressed, bias against unions, and possible history of firing workers who try to organize. Entrepreneur-managers often stated that they preferred to deal directly with employees rather than through workers' representatives. These entrepreneurs also tended not to join employers' organizations, which may indicate their general belief that the enterprise should avoid outside interference of any sort, making it more difficult for them to accept workers' views that affiliating with an outside trade union could improve employment relations within a firm.

Even if anti-union pressure is not explicit, subtle pressure may exist in the more personal and paternalistic relationship between the entrepreneur and workers, such that management may consider an attempt to organize as a personal affront. This is particularly true in cases where the entrepreneur has close ties to the community and there is a tradition of paternalism rather than unionization. In such cases, the presence of a union may be interpreted by the community as failure on the part of the entrepreneur to fulfil his or her paternalistic role effectively. Closer proximity may also enable the employer to detect and address issues and concerns more quickly so that workers do not feel that a union is necessary. The link between the entrepreneur and the community may reinforce the personal and paternalistic relationship and make employers less inclined to support the presence of a union for fear of being stigmatized in the community.

In order to discourage or prevent organization, entrepreneurs with strong anti-union views may hire workers who cannot organize, or who are less inclined to do so. Suddha Vanaspati hires a high percentage of foreign workers, who do not have the right under national law to join a trade union, as a strategy for undermining workers' efforts to organize. Another enterprise hires exclusively young women for most of its operations, in part because they are less inclined to organize.

The use of high rates of temporary workers in SMEs may also deter workers from organizing. In some countries, national law does not extend the right to join a trade union to temporary or seasonal workers. Even when such workers do have the right, those who would like to obtain a more stable position may be less inclined to organize against the employer's wishes for fear of not being hired again. And those with regular contracts know that they can be replaced easily by someone from the pool of experienced seasonal workers. This consideration is particularly strong in a labour-surplus economy, as was the case in the four countries in our study. Nonetheless, non-permanent status is not always a barrier to organizing (see box 7). And in the case of Dagatyaman, most of the seasonal workers were relatives of regular workers, and hence less likely to replace them.

Workers who are interested in organizing may not have sufficient support from the relevant union or confederation, owing to the union's lack of capacity to organize in smaller firms, which can be very time-consuming. This was the case at Twikki Meat in Botswana. National union officials visited the factory to encourage workers to form a union. However, they did not follow

Box 7    Contract status not always an impediment to organizing: Mitho Chau Chau Foods

Mitho Chau Chau has 170 staff. Only ten workers have permanent status; the other 94 per cent of the workforce are either temporary or contract workers. In addition, the enterprise employs 300 daily wage earners for 12-month periods, after which they may be upgraded to temporary staff. In this company management is top-down with no worker participation. Yet workers have been partially successful in organizing. Ninety-seven workers have joined one trade union confederation, which management has recognized. Fifty workers have joined another, although management does not want to recognize the smaller union and there have been no elections to determine the authorized trade union. A committee comprised of five representatives from each of the two trade unions has been formed to bargain collectively with management, and workers often approach either of the trade unions to help solve individual problems with management. Union members meet regularly, albeit only outside the factory premises. As a result of collective bargaining, the unions have been able to secure some benefits and improvements in working conditions.

up the visit, and workers had no idea what to do themselves. The enterprise remains unorganized.

Not surprisingly, the attitudes and actions of both workers and managers have influenced the desire and ability of workers to organize effectively in the small enterprises studied (see box 8). Workers' views were not always homogenous within an enterprise, although negative stereotypes and prejudices dominated in the 12 enterprises studied. For instance, in the three Kenyan firms the workers had the legal right to organize. In two of them, Maziwa and Ugali Tamu, the workers used to have recognition agreements with a confederation, but later withdrew from the unions. About a third of the workers interviewed felt that the unions were not useful and that their activities could lead to job losses. They preferred to have direct dialogue on terms and conditions of employment with management rather than going through unions; and they felt that the unions were not best placed to represent them as they also had their own interests to pursue. However, over 70 per cent of those interviewed believed that unions were the best placed institutions to champion workers' rights, that they boosted the workers' bargaining power, and that they should be maintained. Workers in the third enterprise, Mchuzi Safi, are members of a union. Management in all three firms expressed negative views of unions, stating that workers who join them develop divided loyalties which harm productivity. The newly established Productivity Centre of Kenya is helping to change perceptions about trade unions and raise awareness of the positive impact they can have on enterprise performance.

Even though the majority of workers in the small firms studied chose, for various reasons, to remain unorganized, unions still had an important though indirect influence on employment relations. The small firms studied all applied the provisions of the labour code, particularly with respect to the adoption of the minimum wage and other conditions of work. In most countries, and specifically in the countries represented in this study, the labour code is developed through tripartite consultation involving workers' and employers' organizations. Hence unions have contributed to the improvement of conditions of work in these firms even when there is no enterprise-level representation. Evidence suggests that collective bargaining at regional levels also has an indirect influence that improves the wages and conditions of work in unorganized enterprises.

Furthermore, the opposition of management to unionization may benefit workers when the right to organize is nonetheless respected, because it gives management a strong incentive to take the needs and concerns of workers into account. Of course, strong protection of the right to form a trade union, in law and in practice, is an essential precondition. In one firm studied, management acknowledged that, although it did not prevent workers from

Box 8     The difference an attitude can make: Two examples from Nepal

Two firms in Nepal provide good examples of the interrelationship of worker and employer attitudes towards workers' organizations.

At Suddha Vanaspati workers are organized. However, management views trade unions as a problem-creating group which encourages strikes, lock-outs and other disturbances in the company. Management strongly resisted workers' efforts to organize, so much so that the workers won a judgement in court against management to reinstate the organizers who were wrongfully dismissed. Due to the acrimony surrounding that bitter dispute, the organizers chose not to return to the enterprise, leaving a vacuum in leadership for the workers, while management hostility to unions became further entrenched. Another group of workers has since organized and been recognized by management, but there is no positive benefit to either party. There are no worker welfare committees, and workers meet mostly outside the workplace on an informal basis, with little effect. Labour–management relations in the enterprise are poor, and likely to remain that way. Management thinks that the union is controlled more by external politics than by the needs of its members; and the trade union believes that company accounts showing losses are simply a means of evading taxes and ignoring workers' demands for improvements in wages, working conditions, and payment of bonuses. Because of the lack of trust between management and unions, there is no effort by either side to improve labour–management cooperation and productivity.

This low-trust environment creates a lose–lose situation. Workers work continuously for eight hours in poor facilities with scant concern for occupational health and safety; and they receive only minimum wages and the barest of benefits. The company has failed to adapt effectively to decreased market access. And it hasn't been able to increase productivity or create new market niches. The financial performance of the company is poor, and shares with a face value of Rs100 just a few years ago are now trading at Rs62.

In contrast, management and workers at Shikhar Maida view each other more positively and hence have a more harmonious and cooperative relationship. In this enterprise, initial efforts to organize workers in 1980 were met with resistance, and the workers went on strike. Nonetheless, the union was established without further opposition. The first collective bargaining agreement was reached after a five-day strike in 1982. Subsequent agreements have been reached by consensus, without strikes, which is significant given that work disruptions are typical in collective bargaining in Nepal. Relations have grown sufficiently positive that the company has been able to restructure with the cooperation of the union, providing voluntary retirement packages for 60 staff. This company's performance is competitive for the sub-sector.

forming a trade union, it actively discouraged organization by granting benefits and assistance to employees, and creating channels of direct and frequent worker access to top management. The wage and benefits package for these workers was above that required by law. Evidence from this small study indicates that effective legal protection for workers' right to form associations plays an important role in conditions of work and labour–management partnership in small enterprises, even in enterprises where workers choose to remain unorganized.

## Membership in employers' organizations

Entrepreneurs in the vast majority of firms studied did not belong to an employers' organization. Only three firms, Mchuzi Safi and Maziwa in Kenya, and Shikhar Maida in Nepal, were members. There is not enough information in the cases to provide an educated guess as to why the others did not feel association was worthwhile.

The firms which did join the local employers' organization had quite differing approaches to labour–management cooperation. At Maziwa there was no trade union but management stated that it was not opposed to having one. Mchuzi Safi has recognized a union but management is very hostile to it. On the other hand, Shikhar Maida has a recognized union, and the representatives and management work together in a constructive partnership (see box 9). Therefore, although there was a strong correlation in the small sample between entrepreneurs' respect for workers' right to join a trade union and their ability to develop cooperation in the workplace, there was no correlation between an entrepreneur's own participation in an organization and his or her respect for the right of workers to form a trade union or willingness to work with union representatives.

# Conclusion

The human resources policy in small firms, whether formal or informal, is to a considerable extent driven or influenced by a number of considerations. Clearly there is a conscious effort to put in place human resources management policies and practices that motivate workers to contribute to enterprise performance. The scope and mechanisms for achieving this objective vary substantially, but the majority see at least some connection between good practices concerning recruitment, training and development, safety and health, and good wages and benefits on the one hand, and cooperation and partnership on the other, as an important means for improving enterprise productivity and competitiveness. These observed tendencies are consistent with findings by other researchers, such as Kinnie et al. (1999).

Firms often adopted a mixture of a more professional human resources management strategy and informal human resources management practices with the aim of preserving flexibility to respond quickly to change. This mixed approach to the employment relationship represents a fusion of a familial

Box 9    Trade union contribution to productivity improvement: Shikar Maida

Management at Shikhar Maida originally opposed the formation of a trade union and did not try to develop a cooperative relationship, which consequently limited the trade union's ability to contribute to the enterprise.  However, the trade union and management were both forced to reconsider their working relationship, following a financial crisis at the mill.  Each side committed itself to solving problems in a more constructive manner, and instituted regular management–union meetings on productivity issues.

Some concrete outcomes of cooperation between management and the trade union include:

- Management was able to introduce two cuts in the workforce through union support of a voluntary retirement programme.

- Following training on clean production, the trade union proposed to have workers be responsible for cleaning the factory themselves, to save on staffing costs.

- Management was able to introduce piece-rate payment of packaging to reduce costs.

- Collective bargaining agreements are reached by consensus without recourse to strikes, which is rare for this sector in Nepal.  There has not been a strike in the enterprise during the last 15 years.

- The rate of accidents is exceptionally low for the industry.

- During a recent national three-day strike, management and the union used the time for holding section-wide labour–management meetings to discuss production issues.

Management states that it appreciates the trade union's role in the enterprise.  For its part, the union states that its priority is ensuring the smooth operation of the mill to preserve and improve its competitive position, particularly vis-à-vis "grey" operators which create "unfair competition".

mode of relation with modern managerial systems, such as the introduction of the appraisal system for objectivity and equity in compensation. This fusion has the potential to help sustain or build cooperation, when the correct balance of interests is struck which is essential for building trust between management and workers.

Industry- or sector-level agreements tend to encourage enterprises to develop more formal human resources management practices. However, SMEs often argue that this bias towards more formal human resources management systems is precisely the difficulty for them in adhering to the agreements. Such difficulty may be due in part to the fact that most are not members of industry employers' associations, or are only marginally associated with them; therefore, they do not have access to the capacity-building services employers' organizations have to offer, and are less likely to participate in forums where they can exchange ideas and learn from other SMEs' experiences in order to help them to apply the provisions of agreements. This sub-optimal equilibrium encourages SMEs to remain with informal human resources management practices.

Yet there are clear advantages to more formal approaches to human resources management, including transparency, consistency, more clearly transmitting expectations and a greater sense of fairness. These attributes can go a long way to helping firms to develop greater labour–management cooperation. Not surprisingly, ambitious firms that are keen to increase productivity, expand markets, and develop new product lines are moving in the direction of developing more formal human resources management procedures.

The small enterprises studied here vary substantially in the importance they place on promoting labour–management cooperation, both directly through developing communication channels and empowering workers to be proactive, and indirectly through general human resources management practices which create the foundation for building trust in an enterprise.

Chapter 5 will take a closer look at some of the factors that seem to be influencing management's decision whether to invest in cultivating labour–management cooperation. A better understanding of the motivations, resources, constraints and difficulties small enterprises face will help in understanding why labour–management cooperation takes a particular form in a small enterprise, and what sorts of interventions could most effectively help SMEs to improve cooperation.

# FACTORS INFLUENCING THE DECISION TO DEVELOP LABOUR–MANAGEMENT COOPERATION IN SMALL AND MEDIUM-SIZED ENTERPRISES 5

Returning to the brief review of literature about labour–management relations in SMEs, the characterization of SMEs as either "good" or "bad" enterprises is an over-simplification. Small firms compete in changing markets, and exist in complex and not always consistent regulatory environments. Furthermore, each small firm has its own unique characteristics, which are often shaped by changing circumstances in a dynamic evolutionary process.

Kochan and Osterman (1994) discuss the impacts of certain factors on the likelihood of an enterprise adopting at least one cooperation-dependent work-place practice (employee participation in problem solving, processes, or TQM practices; team-based work systems and job rotation). They found in their studies that a firm is more likely to adopt at least one of these practices when:

- it is subject to international competition or competes in international markets;

- its competitive strategy emphasizes product and service quality, differentiation, technological innovation and speed to market rather than low cost;

- the skill levels required of the production technology are high;

- management believes that it is appropriate for the enterprise to take responsibility for the personal and family well-being of its employees.

They also identify particular constraints that SMEs face when deciding to invest in promoting labour–management cooperation:

- the higher risks of losing to competitors employees that they have trained;

- the capital and thin margin constraints, which make them reluctant (or unable) to take the risks inherent in changing work organization;

71

- the owner-manager's lack of time to make the required time and effort investments;

- high unemployment and a generally under-trained labour force, which together reduce incentives for owner-managers to invest in social capital.

This chapter will discuss these pressures and constraints faced by the firms studied, and identify which ones appear to have the most influence on management's investment in labour–management cooperation.

# External factors

External factors over which the entrepreneur has relatively little control include market structure, regulation, certification schemes, conditions for market access, and political climate. Although no one factor conclusively determines the extent of labour–management cooperation in an enterprise, and various factors in combination may have conflicting influences, these factors often strongly colour management's view of the importance of cooperation, and whether it is an "affordable" investment.

## Market structure

Market structure can have a substantial impact on management's willingness to invest in building social capital to promote cooperation. New entrants to the market, changes in demand, the opening or closing of markets, and market access requirements such as certification all have a substantial influence on the form and extent of labour–management cooperation in small enterprises. Profound external shocks such as natural disasters can further test relations within an enterprise. Markets with substantial competitive pressures intensify management's inclination to retain as much control and decision-making as possible, and heightens the fear of inflexibility typically associated with a formal approach to human resources management. Although all firms face competitive pressures from market structures, small firms are particularly vulnerable since they are more limited in their ability to reduce costs through economies of scale.

Government economic policy greatly influences local market demand and revenues for operators targeting that market. Sales at Ugali Tamu, which focuses exclusively on the domestic market, have declined in part due to the increase in poverty in the transition phase of market liberalization, which has sharply decreased demand.

On the supply side, the firms studied all operate under substantial, or even intense, market pressures. For instance, Mitho Chau Chau operates in the noodle market, which has so many local and foreign competitors that product prices have remained constant for the last ten years, although the cost of inputs has continued to rise.

For some firms, ease of entry was a great source of competitive pressure. Twikki Meat operates in a sector with strong competition due to a government monopoly on exports that restricts access to foreign markets coupled with relatively easy access to funding for start-ups through a development corporation which encourages continued growth of supply. Even for firms operating in markets with relatively few new entrants, difficulty of entry alone did not necessarily protect the established enterprises. Tebe Mills has few local competitors but faces stiff competition from imports in a market where consumers are well conditioned to buy imports because local mills did not exist for a long time.

Some firms started as monopoly operators, but subsequently lost their advantage. Shikhar Maida started with no competitors but a change in regulations resulted in a flood of new operators. Now 22 mills exist in the sector, all of which have similar technology and capacity, and on average use only half of their capacity.

Even when technology is not initially similar, it is easy enough to copy, forcing producers to constantly upgrade and refine products to keep a competitive edge. For example, Sumsuman Foods developed a market niche by modernizing production and packaging of chicharron (fried chicken skin). Replication by competitors has pushed the company to innovate further.

Enterprises which have never had a monopoly position are still vulnerable to pressures from market liberalization. Maziwa experienced a sharp decline in domestic sales due to market liberalization in 2002, forcing the company to target the European Union market.

Some of the small firms studied are highly concentrated in a specific market and hence are more vulnerable to changes in trade rules. In the ghee market, the Nepalese firm Suddha Vanaspati was previously competitive in India due to tariff differentials on the import of raw materials which favoured the Nepalese producers. But the Indian Government dramatically reduced import quotas, and the Nepalese Government increased tariffs on imports of raw materials, dramatically eroding its competitive position in both the Indian and Nepalese markets. Ugali Tamu, which had previously exported 95 per cent of its products, abruptly lost all foreign market access when the border with Tanzania closed, forcing it to focus on a domestic market strategy.

There was no correlation in the case studies between market competitiveness and investment in cooperation. For example, the four Nepalese firms studied all face great competition in their respective markets, which push profit margins to the minimum. Three of the firms had very low levels of cooperation, or none at all. Management at the fourth firm, Shikhar Maida, has invested heavily in building good relations with the trade union. However, the firm's early entry into the market and established position might have some bearing on its ability to invest.

Among the firms which invested the most in developing cooperation, the critical factor seemed to be the ability to create a market niche which both required investment and enabled them to provide it. For instance, Sumsuman Foods' niche, built around innovative packaging, quality, flavourings and services, has motivated management to invest in cooperation; the shelter the niche provides from fiercer competition has given it the space to take the risks involved in sharing greater decision-making, responsibility and rewards.

## Regulation

In addition to trade regulations shaping market structure, it is often argued that small firms may be affected by competitive pressures arising from excessive regulation, poor or inconsistent enforcement of regulations, or regulation which changes too rapidly (de Soto, 2000). The cases studied lend some support to this assertion, but do not overwhelmingly support it.

For instance, management at Mitho Chau Chau has granted permanent contracts to only ten out of a total of 170 workers because it believes that providing statutory benefits and protection against retrenchment would make it uncompetitive. However, the other three Nepalese firms do not rely on the overwhelming use of casual workers as a means of adapting to regulations concerning benefits and retrenchments.

Several enterprises studied distinguished sharply between a generally competitive market and "unfair competition" from unregistered firms or firms which only partially comply with the law due to poor enforcement of regulations. Managers commonly felt that firms operating outside the law made it much more difficult for them to provide good working conditions as a means of fostering cooperation, and they were more inclined to retain controlling management strategies instead of cultivating trust and partnership. However, not all firms responded the same way: at Shikhar Maida management and trade union representatives identified the threat from unfair competition as the main motivation for cooperating more closely in an effort to remain competitive.

Nonetheless, two aspects of regulation affected the firms in a consistent manner: excessive regulation and rapidly changing regulation, both of which generally resulted in very high compliance costs, particularly for small enterprises. Firms in Nepal stated that the general regulatory environment created stress for small operators, in part because there was too much regulation, and in part because the regulations frequently changed, further increasing the cost of compliance.

## Certification schemes

Although excessive and rapidly changing regulation, as well as inconsistent enforcement, often creates negative pressure on management, regulation tied to foreign market access in the form of certification schemes has a generally positive effect on building cooperation in an enterprise. This is probably due to the existence of a direct benefit in the form of market access, consistent monitoring and enforcement, and stability of the regulatory scheme, all of which make it cost-effective for an enterprise to invest in social capital, with a clear and immediate return on that investment.

Those firms studied which are pursuing an aggressive market expansion strategy focused on high-end domestic markets or export markets are generally required to meet more exacting quality- and product- specification standards. To meet these higher standards they aim to adopt and install recognized systems such as ISO 9000 and HACCP for the food-processing industry (similar certification schemes exist for other industries). These quality-management standards apply total quality management (TQM) principles which involve employees at all levels as one of the key foundations, and require firms to develop participatory systems and build the competencies of managers and workers through in-house and off-factory training. In some cases, the efforts to meet ISO 9000 and HACCP requirements are reinforced by other participatory programmes such as 5S and Quality Control Circle (QCC).

The ISO 9000 family of quality-management system standards is based on a set of 8 principles that includes involvement of people and the process of continuous improvement (see box 10).

The principle concerning involvement of people (ISO 9000, 2000, no.3) states that people at all levels are the essence of an organization and that their full involvement enables their abilities to be applied for the benefit of the organization. Applying this principle leads to people:

- understanding the importance of their contribution and role in the organization;
- identifying the constraints on their performance;
- accepting ownership of problems and their responsibility for solving them;
- evaluating their performance against their personal goals and objectives;

**Box 10    ISO 9000: Quality management principles**

1 Customer focus

2 Leadership

3 Involvement of people

4 Process approach

5 Systems approach to management

6 Continual improvement

7 Factual approach to decision-making

8 Mutually beneficial supplier relationship

Source: International Organization for Standardization, 2000. See www.iso.org and www.isoeasy.org

- actively seeking opportunities to enhance their competence, knowledge and experience;
- sharing knowledge and experience;
- openly discussing problems and issues.

HACCP (Hazard Analysis and Critical Control Point) is a systematic approach to the identification, evaluation, and control of food safety hazards. It involves seven principles (USFDA, 2001):

- Analyse hazards: Potential hazards associated with food and measures to control those hazards are identified.
- Identify critical control points: These are points in a food's production – from its raw state through processing and shipping to consumption by consumers – where the potential hazard can be controlled or eliminated.
- Establish preventive measures with critical limits for each control point.
- Establish procedures to monitor the critical control points.
- Establish corrective actions to be taken when monitoring shows that a critical limit has not been met.
- Establish procedures to verify that the system is working properly.
- Establish effective record keeping to document the HACCP system.

Those firms that had ISO 9000 certification showed lower levels of cooperation, but the cooperation which did exist was clearly linked to the principles. For instance, Taja Bakery has ISO 9000 certification. The level of communication and cooperation is relatively poor, owing to its hiring strategy that focuses exclusively on young women, whom management believes to be more compliant. Nonetheless, working conditions are relatively good and some communication channels exist, as a result of management's effort to engage workers in the ISO process. Cooperation could be much higher at Taja Bakery, but without ISO certification it would undoubtedly be lower.

The HACCP application guidelines identify a number of prerequisite programmes upon which the HACCP system should be built. These prerequisite programmes relate to facilities, supplier control, specifications, equipment, pest control and other important areas in ensuring the safety of a food item along its production–distribution and consumption process. The prerequisite programme relating to training encourages and supports involvement of people at all stages of the process. All employees should receive training in personal hygiene, good manufacturing practices (GMP), cleaning and sanitation procedures, personal safety and their role in the HACCP system. It is recognized that the success of a HACCP system depends on educating and training management and employees on the importance of their role in producing safe food and that employees must first understand what HACCP is and then learn the skills necessary to make the system function properly (see USFDA, 2001, 2005; Pearson and Dutson, 2001).

All the firms surveyed which participate in the HACCP certification schemes had good working conditions, numerous communication channels, higher levels of employee input and decision-making and better labour–management relations. For example, Dagatyaman has HACCP certification, which has motivated and guided the firm to establish a more advanced system of cooperation (see box 11).

Firms seriously considering ISO or HACCP certification were also figuring out ways to upgrade their management systems, including improving communication and cooperation. Sumsuman Foods is seeking HACCP certification and has established several of the prerequisite programmes, including Good Manufacturing Practices and Good Sanitation Practices. It invests heavily in developing the competencies of workers and managers, and in fostering labour–management cooperation so that the programmes run as effectively as possible. Sumsuman Foods also has invested extensively in upgrading its human resources management system, including aligning benefits more closely with the needs and wishes of the workers, and establishing a range of gain-sharing programmes.

However, certification is not a guarantee of more advanced labour–management cooperation. For example, Mitho Chau Chau has ISO 9001

Box 11     Impact of HACCP certification requirements on labour–management cooperation: Dagatyaman Seafoods

Dagatyaman Seafoods in the Philippines provides an example of the impact of certification schemes on labour–management cooperation.

The vision of Dagatyaman is to move ahead of the competition by providing the most reasonably-priced, globally accepted quality seafood products anywhere in the market. The enterprise continuously seeks to gain widespread acceptance in the global market, and has implemented a business strategy based on expanding its product range and focusing almost entirely on export markets. Ninety per cent of the company's exports are to the United States, which requires HACCP certification.

The HACCP team in Dagatyaman is composed of personnel from various areas, such as engineering, production, sanitation, quality assurance and microbiology. Line workers are also a critical part of the team, as they are involved at all critical points in the production process. Worker input is not limited to carrying out tasks, but also includes their input in analysing production, drawing up a flow diagram of the production process, verifying food safety at the critical points, and taking action to remedy any defects in the production process. Labour–management cooperation is essential for meeting the requirements for certification.

As a consequence of the critical role workers play in the HACCP team, they are provided extensive training on all aspects of hygiene, food safety, and quality. This substantial investment in the human capital of line workers is supported by human resource strategies which motivate them to use their skills and encourage them to stay with the firm longer term, and which build social capital. To this end, the firm maintains a core of 50 employees, providing them with good working conditions, wages and benefits. The casual workers employed during high season are mostly relatives of the core workforce, and are provided the opportunity to become core workers when there are vacancies.

As part of its HACCP certification programme, Dagatyaman also fosters strong backward and forward linkages in the supply chain. A key component of food safety in the seafoods sub-sector is to ensure quality and hygiene through speedy processing of catches. Consequently, it provides substantial support to its suppliers by entering into exclusive buying arrangements with fishermen without inter-mediaries, including them in some of their management training programmes, and providing them cash advances and personal loans to smooth their income. Dagatyaman also has invested substantially in its relations with distributors, in particular its importer for the US market, which also conducts regular audits as required by the HACCP programme.

Access to foreign markets through the HACCP certification scheme has been highly beneficial for Dagatyaman. The firm has continuously expanded its plant facilities, doubling capacity between 2000 and 2003. Since the current owner took over in 1999, gross sales almost tripled up to 2003.

certification but relies primarily on the most advanced technology to ensure quality in its noodle production business, and in fact has a relatively low level of cooperation. In contrast, several firms without certification nonetheless had relatively high levels of cooperation. For example, Twikki Meat does not have certification because it focuses on the domestic market where it is not required. Nonetheless, the firm has invested in building cooperation because it implements just-in-time production methods, which require high levels of cooperation, to ensure the highest quality and food safety.

## Other external pressures

Workers and managers interviewed identified several other issues, including market access and political climate, that place additional stress on small enterprises. Infrastructure was a major problem for many of the small companies studied, particularly in Botswana and Kenya. For instance, Mchuzi Safi, Maziwa and Ugali Tamu all complained of the poor infrastructure and unreliable water and power supplies, which raise costs, hamper delivery and impair production expansion.

Small firms, with less bargaining power vis-à-vis their larger competitors, also face greater difficulties in obtaining high-quality inputs at a reasonable cost. Firms in Kenya especially complained about the high cost and poor quality of raw materials.

Political climate can have a tremendous impact on firms. Some companies in Nepal complained of the effect of political instability, which adversely affects their ability to raise capital to upgrade and expand production. In Kenya workers noted that the change in government has brought greater democracy and participation in general, but the growing role of civil society has undermined the position of trade unions, creating a greater imbalance in worker–manager relations in the enterprise. But again, it is not just the pressure but management's response which mattered. In the case of Mitho Chau Chau, managers used the political instability as an excuse to ignore management problems and poor performance, but management in the other three Nepalese firms did not.

Of course disasters, natural or otherwise, can also wipe out market demand or supply, with smaller firms being disproportionately harmed. However, such pressure does not always have a negative effect on cooperation. In the Philippines, a tree blight eliminated Masapat Farms' charcoal production; and the eruption of Mt. Pinatubo and the Asian financial crisis temporarily wiped out much of the market demand for its remaining product lines. Management's response was to rely more on cooperative management strategies to help diversify the product line and build a market niche.

Enterprises seek to reach and sustain an equilibrium – a state where it feels that it is strong enough to retain control when reacting to external factors and events rather than simply being blown around by them. Sometimes external factors overwhelm an enterprise and leave little or no choice for management in how to respond. More often than not, however, as we saw in the above examples, adverse changes in market structure, regulations, or other events such as increased political instability or growing poverty of consumers, can be adjusted for internally, by altering business and management strategies which an enterprise does control.

# Internal factors

Studies of SME management systems and practices stress the inseparability of the owner-manager and the small enterprise. In micro and small enterprises the locus of control typically rests with one individual who usually makes most, if not all, of the important decisions. Therefore, the thinking goes, the personality of the entrepreneur is the driving force behind labour–management cooperation in small firms.

Not all the firms studied fit this model, and those that do only partially support this claim. In general, the cases examined suggest that a complex combination of internal factors unique to each firm together influence management's willingness to invest in social capital.

Internal factors shaping labour–management cooperation include the ownership structure, financial structure, management structure, the motivation and mission of the enterprise, the competencies of managers and workers, proximity and the business and management strategies pursued. Of course, these factors are not entirely independent of the entrepreneur's personality and preferences, and indeed are shaped at least partly by them. Nonetheless, these factors can have a more direct impact on labour–management cooperation, independent of the entrepreneur's idiosyncrasies.

## Ownership, financing and management structure

In theory, the structures of ownership, financing and the management of a small enterprise should have a substantial impact on the willingness of the management to cultivate cooperation. The ownership structure determines the sources of initial financing and greatly influences ongoing access to capital for upgrading and expanding. The financial structure, in turn, determines the exposure to risk for each owner and, potentially, the degree to which the ownership and management structures overlap.

When most or all of the wealth of the entrepreneur (and often that of other immediate family members) is tied up in the enterprise, this concentrates the entrepreneur's exposure to risk. At the same time, small enterprises are more vulnerable to market forces because they have a smaller and more concentrated client base and less diversified production. Arguably, an owner-manager is inclined to mitigate the risk-taking inherent in entrepreneurship with risk aversion in the daily operation of a young enterprise. Hence he or she is more likely to closely control all aspects of production. Under these circumstances, it is much more typical to find very close, or complete, overlap of the ownership and management structures.

However, separate management and ownership structures do not guarantee a higher level of cooperation in a firm. Mitho Chau Chau is an example of a family-owned company which is professionally managed by an outside group, yet cooperation is virtually non-existent.

With limited resources, small enterprises are less able to provide attractive jobs and social protections such as pensions and health care, although this is not uniformly the case (Sengenberger et al, 1990). Consequently, small enterprises have more difficulty attracting and retaining skilled workers. The small enterprise generally relies on the technical knowledge of the entrepreneur-manager, a technical partner or key and experienced employees, thus limiting its capacity for innovation and upgrading of processes and product quality, and exposing the firm to risk of loss of that technical capacity.

This limited resource base also means that small enterprises typically lack the funds to hire independent managers or administrators until they reach a certain level of development. Consequently, the entrepreneur and family must carry out the tasks of practically all the functional areas (marketing, finance, personnel, production, and so on) and even perform some of the jobs on the production floor, all in addition to the day-to-day handling of transactional and other relationships with customers, marketing channels, suppliers, bankers, regulatory authorities, peers, friends, family and other stakeholders in the business environment (Gibb, 1997). While this enables the entrepreneur-manager to have a holistic view of the business, it also places tremendous demands on him or her and makes it very difficult to be away from the business for an extended period of time.

Furthermore, as Jennings and Beaver (1997) argue, without separate management a small firm's human resources management process cannot be separated from the personality and experience of the person running the business. Having staff specifically dedicated to human resources management in an enterprise has the advantage of creating distance from the owner's personality and preferences, which may not always be consistent and trans-parent, and daily personnel practices. Human resources management can then move from ad hoc problem-solving to responses guided by policy which can be more consciously and consistently tied to business objectives.

The cases largely support this proposition. Those firms which had dedicated human resources managers generally had higher levels of cooperation, with one exception. Mitho Chau Chau, as we have seen, was professionally managed with a dedicated human resources department, yet had a very low level of cooperation.

The financial structure of a firm may shape management's willingness to separate human resources management from ownership. In firms with a broader base for capital and less concentrated risk, owners may be more inclined to take the risk of letting go of full control over personnel matters. In addition, firms which are less capital-constrained, which is generally the case when the sources of capital are more diversified, are better able to afford dedicated staff.

Evidence from the cases is somewhat mixed. At both Tebe Mills and Twikki Meat, the entrepreneur had relatively easy access to capital and did not bear all of the risk but was subsidized by the government through its development corporation; and in both firms there was a relatively high level of cooperation. However, in the case of Sumsuman Foods and Dagatyaman the entrepreneurs bore the whole risk and still invested in developing cooperation, so these firms do not support the proposition that concentrated risk will make an entrepreneur less inclined to risk developing a cooperative management strategy; but they do support the idea that access to capital also helps to encourage cooperation by allowing entrepreneurs to focus on longer time horizons, since they both have good access to credit and are less capital-constrained than some of the other firms studied.

Two of the twelve firms studied were financed by issuing shares. Suddha Vanaspati was established as a publicly held company, with a state-owned enterprise as one of its main financial backers. Shikhar Maida too was set up as a publicly held enterprise, but three companies own 99 per cent of the shares. In both cases, the ownership and management structures are completely separate, although the shareholders retain some say in the direction of management since there are so few of them. The management structure in each firm consists of a board of directors, a managing director, a general manager, department heads and work teams. Each enterprise has a separate human resources department. In addition, publicly held companies are subject to greater scrutiny through accounting and reporting requirements; this reduces scope for cutting costs through disregarding regulations, evading taxes, and so on. Such pressure can motivate management to upgrade its human resources strategies and to invest in building cooperation as a competitive advantage; but such an outcome is not inevitable, as the two publicly held enterprises in the study indicate (see box 12).

Of course, the stage of development of the firm makes a substantial difference. Most young enterprises continue financing operations mainly

> **Box 12    Contrasting approaches of two publicly held companies to investing in cooperation**
>
> Suddha Vanaspati and Shikhar Maida are two publicly held firms in Nepal with completely opposite approaches to investing in cooperation.
>
> Management at Suddha Vanaspati is not interested in developing cooperation between workers and managers, and the little cooperation that used to exist has eroded. Indeed, management is so keen to avoid cooperation that it has switched its entire production strategy. When the company lost access to the Indian market for ghee, it developed the concept of "build to store" in which it invested heavily in large storage capacity in order to periodically produce large quantities of ghee using casual labourers who are then laid off when storage capacity is filled. This has lead to even worse conditions of work for the staff, a further weakening of the trade union, and worse labour–management relations; cooperation is nearly non-existent.
>
> In contrast, management at Shikhar Maida has made cooperation a key component of its change management strategy. Shikhar Maida is a joint venture between a state-owned company and a semi-public company, and its output goes almost exclusively to supply the parent companies. Its shares are publicly traded, but are held primarily by the founding institutions. When the mill lost its monopoly on production of flour in Nepal, management decided to develop a more constructive relationship with the trade union in order to maintain its competitive position.
>
> It should be noted that Shikhar Maida differs from Suddha Vanaspati in part because it enjoys a captive market – it was established to supply its parent companies which are responsible for marketing and distribution of the milled flour. This may be a significant factor that helped management to feel secure enough to work more constructively with the trade union.

based on the resources of the entrepreneur and his or her family during the period in which the firm generates little or no profit. This narrow resource base encourages management to focus on the short-term, day-to-day operations of the enterprise, and limits or discourages long-term strategic orientation. Management becomes primarily an adaptive process concerned with adjusting a limited amount of resources in order to gain the maximum immediate and short-term advantages, and where efforts are concentrated not on predicting but on controlling the operating environment, adapting as quickly as possible to the changing demands of that environment and devising suitable tactics for mitigating the consequences of any changes that occur (Jennings and Beaver, 1996). This short-term strategy makes entrepreneurs less inclined to invest in social capital which may take a while to realize a return on the investment.

However, attitudes to management control often evolve as the enterprise becomes stronger and more financially viable. As the firm repays its debt for the initial capitalization, it is able to pay more of its operating expenses out of its receipts; it needs to borrow less for ongoing investments and hence becomes less exposed to a risk of defaulting on the loan and losing the enterprise. This creates the psychological space most entrepreneurs need to shift from short-term to medium-term strategic thinking about human resources management. It also creates the financial conditions to employ qualified people dedicated solely to human resources management, and to begin improving conditions of work as a vital component of building cooperation.

The cases generally indicate a relationship between the age of the enterprise and the level of cooperation in an enterprise. However, the causality was not very clear. As firms became financially more stable, they also tended to expand production and increase staff size, motivating the firm to develop specialized management functions. As mentioned above, a management structure with dedicated human resources staff tended to be more committed to developing cooperation. Furthermore, in one case a relatively young enterprise started with a more long-term strategic horizon. Family-owned Sumsuman Foods was founded only in 2001. Nonetheless, the firm has, from the outset, invested heavily in a more formal and professionalized approach to human resources management.

## Motivation and mission

The motivation of the founders may have a strong influence on the development of labour-management cooperation in an enterprise. The founder's entrepreneurial traits such as creativity, achievement, motivation, and perseverance, combined with personal idiosyncrasies such as attitude to structure and standards, view of the environment, and need for recognition strongly influence the way the business is organized and managed. The criteria he or she uses to define business success stem from his or her personal goals, motives and reasons for undertaking the business. For example, while many would consider profitability, expansion and growth to be the best measures of business success, some artisan entrepreneur-managers may prefer to keep the business small and simple to maintain personal control, have a high degree of freedom and allow for more artistic expression. These traits tend to favour a concentration of control and decision-making, which evolves out of the entrepreneur's desire to realize his or her vision and goals for the enterprise.

The conventional wisdom concerning SMEs is that the prospect of being the key or sole decision-maker is a strong motivating factor for many entrepreneurs; hence many studies of labour–management relations in SMEs focus on the personality of the entrepreneur. Our study did not wholly support this view, as the desire to be the boss was cited as a motive in only one case.

More common motives included: the need for employment in the community, a good business opportunity arose, or the company was established as a subsidiary of another company. In two cases, Dagatyaman Seafoods and Tebe Mills, the entrepreneurs sought alternative means of using their professional training: the owner of Tebe Mills wanted to apply her knowledge of nutrition to milling; and the owner of Dagatyaman is a marine biologist. In three cases – Maziwa, Tebe Mills and Ugali Tamu – the owner cited the desire to contribute to the country's food security or safety as a motivating factor.

There is no mention of workers in any of the cited motives, except indirectly in one case, Twikki Meat, where the owner cited the desire to generate employment in the community.

On the other hand, except for one reference to the desire to be the boss, also made by the owner of Twikki Meat, there were no motives cited which hinted at a predisposition against cooperation. Therefore, we cannot say anything about the influence of the founders' motives on the willingness to invest in building cooperation.

The mission of the enterprise – how it views itself and its purpose – can play a key role in shaping labour–management cooperation, particularly when linked to the business strategy of the firm (discussed below). Although the mission statement may be closely related to the motivation of the entrepreneur, it may be formulated by management independent of the owner, and may evolve over time. In firms with professional or quasi-professional management which are trying to move towards more formal management systems, in particular firms with specialized human resources managers, the mission statement often serves to distance management strategies from the entrepreneur's personality and individual (and often inconsistent) preferences. Although this move towards formality may introduce limits to management's flexibility and control, it also may provide additional space to foster cooperation when the entrepreneur is not predisposed to do so.

Of the firms studied, those which expressed a strong customer focus in their mission statements also had the highest levels of cooperation. For example, Sumsuman Foods has the mission to be acknowledged as a prime mover in the Philippines food industry and to be recognized as the company providing the best value for money to customers both locally and abroad. Dagatyaman sets as its mission to provide the most reasonably priced, globally accepted quality seafood products anywhere in the market. Both firms have invested heavily in cultivating a high level of cooperation.

Oddly, the two mission statements that refer to the contribution of workers have low levels of cooperation. Mitho Chau Chau's stated mission is to provide highly nutritious products with the support of its highly qualified, experienced and motivated team. However, it pursues a strategy which relies more heavily on technology than on good relations with employees. The other firm which mentions the role of workers in its mission statement, Ugali Tamu, aims to produce the best quality of pre-packaged grains in the local market through its competent staff. However, the company has invested little in developing cooperation.

One firm, Taja Bakery, considers staff health and safety itself to be part of its mission. It defines as its mission to foster high customer satisfaction focusing on product quality and variety, together with staff health and safety, through continuous improvement in technology and management. However, this has not translated into a cooperation-based management style. The firm has very little cooperation, although it does have exceptional safety measures such as providing sleeping quarters so that night-shift workers do not have to commute in the dark.

## Proximity

Proximity – the extent of frequent interaction between workers and managers – is determined by management decisions concerning staff size and growth rate, and locations of production and management.

Research and arguments surrounding the issue of proximity and its impact on labour-management cooperation are the most lively and contentious, in part because proximity, more than any other attribute, epitomizes the small firm. The owner-manager of a small enterprise generally is in much closer daily contact with the workers (Brown et al., 1990).

Conventional wisdom on labour–management relations in SMEs which has dominated the thinking of management and policy-makers in the past is that labour–management relations are relatively harmonious in small enterprises because of the close proximity of workers and the owner-manager, in many cases the owner-manager knowing every worker by name. This has been attributed to the close and regular direct contact between the manager and workers, and informal and personal supervision and control which open up the possibility for effective communication channels. More regular interaction also has the potential to strengthen relations between workers and the employer and hence to promote a spirit of cooperation, mutual respect and moral attachment. And the "family atmosphere" of family-owned small enterprises give the worker a sense of belonging and a reason to identify with the firm. Therefore, it has been argued, workers in SMEs have sought employment there because they value such a collegial environment and have a different attitude to work; this explains the observed lower levels of industrial action and lower rates of trade unionism compared with larger firms.

There are two problems with this theory. First, as noted above, small firms face a multitude of internal and external forces inclining owner-managers towards greater concentration of control and away from labour–management cooperation. The firms studied indicate that not all small firms opt for a more cooperative style of management. Second, the "evidence" of good labour–management relations in small firms – the ability of small firms to attract and retain workers despite generally lower wages and conditions of work; lower rates of industrial action; and lower rates of trade union membership – may have little or nothing to do with management efforts to promote cooperation. For instance, the ability to recruit and retain workers may be due more to the worker's limited employment options than to any sense of personal commitment to the firm. A study of workers in Japanese SMEs showed that work in an SME was considered more satisfying and humanizing (ILO, 1997, p. 7). Yet a study of workers in British SMEs showed that there was no difference in attitude or level of commitment between people working in small firms and other workers; rather, workers in SMEs tended to be there simply because there were limited options elsewhere owing to their lack of skills, a slack labour market, or inability to relocate to other options (Goss, 1991, p. 72).

Researchers such as Rainnie (1989) reject the argument that closer proximity leads to better labour–management cooperation in small enterprises. Rainnie argues that any potential benefits of proximity to encourage cooperation are swamped by the level of dependence of the producer on a small number of large customers who are able to squeeze margins enough to force the producer to pursue a low-cost strategy focusing on labour costs.

Although a small enterprise generally is "restricted in economic, technical, personnel and political resources, and [lacks] the ability and the autonomy to influence the external business environment" (Sengenberger et al., 1990, p. 199), this does not necessarily imply that small firms are so affected by outsiders that they are forced to adopt a lowest cost strategy at the expense of labour–management cooperation. As Marlow (2001) explains, not all SMEs are in such a state of dependency, and even those who do rely on relatively few customers do not necessarily adopt a low-cost strategy because their clients are concerned not only with cost but also with quality, timeliness, reliability and flexibility. In other words, buyers seek the most overall productive firm rather than the cheapest.

The firms studied were all at the top of the value chain, and either distributed their produce directly or on consignment with individuals or retail outlets. The exception was Shikhar Maida, which supplied almost exclusively to its parent companies. Hence, the firms studied did not have pressure from large buyers with strong bargaining power, which supports Marlow's view.

Furthermore, as discussed earlier, the firms studied generally complied with all legal requirements for conditions of work and benefits, and often went beyond these requirements, indicating that although being competitive on cost was important, it was not an overwhelming factor which impaired the firms' ability to develop cooperation, since about half did develop moderate or high levels of cooperation, and only a few firms were at the very low end of the continuum. This also seems to support more the arguments of Sengenberger et al., and Marlow than those of Rainnie.

In Marlow's view, the blurring of functions of an entrepreneur-manager and the close daily interaction with workers create the conditions for increased labour–management cooperation, yet these same conditions also make any disciplinary action more complicated since it conflicts with the team spirit the entrepreneur is trying to cultivate. Therefore, in order to deal with infractions in a way which does not disrupt the team, the manager must minimize the risk of infractions in the first instance, and failing that, remove the "problem" person to avoid the spread of hostilities. This creates an environment where "fitting in", i.e., conforming, is very important, which can lead to discrimination issues.

Reaching a similar conclusion, a literature review of studies of small enterprises in European Union member States reports that informal management in close proximity to the workers tends to result in, inter alia, stronger biases in hiring and work assignment, influenced by family and community ties (European Foundation, 2001). The cases clearly support this finding. As discussed in Chapter 4, most of the firms studied recruited workers from the community in which the enterprise operates, drawing on networks of family members, friends, and neighbours, particularly for positions requiring unskilled and semi-skilled workers. Although a community network strategy has many advantages, the main justification given by most enterprise owners for depending on community networks for recruitment was their sense of obligation to contribute to the social and economic development of the community in which they operate.

One way of reconciling these competing views is to look not only at proximity within the small firm but also proximity of the firm to the community in which it is situated. Based on empirical research for small enterprises in the United Kingdom, Goss (1991) concludes that the level of cooperation between the entrepreneur and workers in a small firm will depend on how much the employer depends on the employees (that is, how difficult they are to replace), and the ability of the worker to resist control (how much shirking, protesting and so on he or she can exercise). The greater the dependence of the employer and the greater the ability of the worker to resist control, the more the employer will seek to foster cooperation. If the worker can be easily replaced and therefore is unable to resist control, the community's influence becomes important in shaping management efforts to foster cooperation in those cases where the entrepreneur values his or her relationship with the community.

The cases support this view. The skill levels of the workers in the firms studied were almost uniformly very low. Most workers had only a primary education, and were trained on the job within a short period of time. And all of the firms operated in markets with surplus labour. At the same time, all the firms valued their ties to the community. In addition to using recruitment as a means of bonding with the community, firms such as Tebe Mills and Ugali Tamu were motivated by concern for the food security of the community. Others such as Twikki Meat showed flexibility, allowing permanent workers with farms to be absent for a period during harvest time, and giving temporary employment to community members who replaced them. Twikki Meat also builds relations with the community and customer base by providing low-cost meat packages to low-income people as a community service.

However, the community's influence on a firm's willingness to invest in developing cooperation was not always positive. On the one hand, the *kgotla* system in Botswana, where the community serves as a medium for consultation and advice for decisions as well as dissemination of information, has been incorporated into the management systems of both Tebe Mills and Twikki Meat, and both firms sit towards the high end of the continuum. On the other, changing community perceptions of trade unions in Kenya have encouraged the Kenyan firms in the study to stop investing in developing cooperation with workers, through their representatives or otherwise. All three Kenyan firms are at the lower end of the continuum.

In several cases ties to suppliers, distributors and customers were also very important, and often linked to strengthening community ties. Maziwa has developed strong backward linkages with its suppliers, which are also part of the community in which it is located, by helping farmers to organize into cooperatives. Ugali Tamu strengthens its ties to the community by sourcing locally whenever possible, and is in the process of helping local rice farmers to organize into a cooperative to help decrease the prevalence of hunger among the producers during shortfalls in production. Sumsuman Foods uses local sourcing as a means of strengthening community ties. Twikki Meat and Masapat Farms also source locally and ensure their suppliers receive quick and timely cash payments, which is very important to the survival of local farmers and their families. And Dagatyaman has invested substantially in developing ties with both its suppliers and distributors; it even includes key suppliers in some training on leadership skills. Ugali Tamu and Maziwa are at the lower end of the continuum, while Sumsuman Foods and Dagatyaman are at the high end. This mixed impact indicates that ties with community, suppliers and distributors can serve to either reinforce high levels of labour–management cooperation or partially compensate for lower levels.

## Business strategy

The business strategy of a firm has the single greatest impact on management's willingness to invest in building cooperation. Of course, the other factors discussed, such as market structure, in turn influence a firm's business strategy; but they do not determine it. Management consciously chooses a business strategy, generally linked to its mission statement, and most often has more than one choice available.

A cost-reduction strategy which focuses on reducing wages and benefits as much as possible tends to attract lower-skilled workers with lower productivity, and to increase staff turnover as workers search for better options. As a consequence, a manager pursuing this business strategy is less inclined to share information and consult workers, or invest more broadly in social capital.

A cost-reduction strategy which focuses on trimming non-wage costs tends to have the opposite effect because the workers are the key ally in trimming waste and innovating in production processes. In such a context, the return on investment in social capital is potentially much higher. Tebe Mills provides an example: it focuses on upgrading the nutritional quality of its products and has invested substantially to develop a relatively high level of cooperation.

Similarly, a business strategy which seeks to move the enterprise up the value chain will be much more inclined to cultivate a cooperative relationship between workers and managers since the workers will play a key role in helping the firm to move up. Hence, the firm will rely more on effective channels of communication and cooperation between workers and management for sharing information and increasing workers' commitment to the enterprise. In both cases, management's commitment to a strategy which prioritizes decent wages and conditions of work will predispose workers to respond positively to efforts to increase the social capital of the enterprise. The firms in the study which competed in the higher end of domestic markets or foreign markets, such as Dagatyaman, invested heavily in developing cooperation, in part to obtain the certification typically required for market access.

Of course, strategies may be mixed, such as simultaneously reducing non-wage costs and moving up the value chain. A given strategy may also be pursued in a variety of ways. For instance, Twikki Meat's approach to customer satisfaction, which was pursued in a way which relied heavily on workers' contributions, may be compared with the approach of Suddha Vanaspati which relied exclusively on customer satisfaction surveys conducted by sales staff and which had limited impact on improving customer satisfaction.

It is also important to stress that the competitiveness strategy of an enterprise is not fixed; it can evolve over time, or change abruptly due to particular incidents or outside forces. A small enterprise may feel compelled initially to minimize wages and benefits while its financial base is still very fragile, perhaps with the owner him- or herself forgoing a wage for a substantial period. As the firm becomes financially more stable and the client base develops, the owner may feel more at liberty to pursue other business strategies.

Sometimes the change is due to a generational change in management of the family-owned enterprise. Twikki Meat is an example of a firm which altered its strategy when the son of the founder finished business school and took over some of the management functions.

Or change may be due to a change in the market structure which makes a particular strategy which has worked for many years suddenly less effective. However low wages and benefits may be in a particular country, the fact of exposing a producer to a competing exporter with even lower labour-related costs or cost of inputs may force that producer to switch to another strategy such as upgrading quality. A good example of this is Shikhar Maida, which lost its monopoly and subsequently decided to work more closely with the trade union to preserve its competitive position in the market.

Business strategies cited by the managers interviewed included: expanding product line, expanding support services, quality and safety, quality through technology, aggressive market expansion, aggressive marketing, modest or no expansion, strong customer orientation, customer satisfaction through surveys, focus on lower end of market, innovation, reduction of waste, brand image and brand development. Table 4 shows the expected and actual impact on cooperation for each of these strategies, for each firm that pursued them.

Of the strategies pursued, the predicted and actual levels of cooperation corresponded completely for eight strategies and was mixed for the remaining four. In very few cases did the predicted and actual levels not correspond at all; of these, some were cases where the level was higher than predicted owing to the simultaneous effect of other strategies. For instance, the observed medium level of cooperation at Twikki Meat, despite pursuing a strategy of non-expansion, can be explained by the simultaneous pursuit of a customer-orientation strategy, which is expected to increase the return on investment.

Table 4  Correlation between business strategy and labour–management cooperation

| General business strategy | Importance of worker contribution | Expected impact on cooperation | Enterprise | Observed cooperation |
|---|---|---|---|---|
| Expanding product line | Workers are a substantial source of ideas | Increased investment | Maziwa<br>Tebe Mills<br>Dagatyaman Seafood<br>Masapat Farms | Modest<br>High<br><br>High<br>Medium |
| Expanding support services | Workers are a key means of delivering services | Increased investment | Sumsuman Foods | High |
| Quality and product safety | Workers play a key role in improvements | Increased investment | Twikki Meat<br>Shikhar Maida<br>Ugali Tamu<br>Maziwa | Medium<br>High<br>Low<br>Low |
| Quality through technology | Can be done with little worker input | None or decrease | Suddha Vanaspati | Low |
| Aggressive market expansion | Can be done without worker contribution | None | Mitho Chau Chau | Low |
| Aggressive marketing | Can be done without worker contribution | None | Maziwa | Low |
| Modest or no expansion | Can be done without worker contribution | Decreased investment | Mchuzi Safi<br>Maziwa<br>Twikki Meat | Low<br>Low<br>Medium |
| Strong customer otrientation | Worker contribution essential for meeting customer expectations, to channel information and to respond most effectively | Increased investment | Twikki Meat<br>Mitho Chau Chau<br>Sumsuman Foods<br>Dagatyaman Seafood | Medium<br>Low<br>High<br><br>High |
| Customer satisfaction through surveys | Can be done without worker contribution | None | Suddha Vanaspati | Low |
| Focus on lower end of market | Worker contribution not necessarily important | Decreased investment | Taja Bakery<br>Mitho Chau Chau | Low<br>Low |
| Innovation | Workers' ideas potentially very important | Increased investment | Taja Bakery<br>Sumsuman Foods | Low<br>High |
| Reduce waste | Worker commitment important | Increased investment | Tebe Mills | High |
| Brand image and brand development | Can be done without worker contribution | None | Mitho Chau Chau<br>Ugali Tamu<br>Dagatyaman Seafood | Low<br>Low<br><br>High |
| Operating more flexibly | Worker commitment essential | Increased investment | Shikhar Maida | High |

For the business strategy focusing on quality and product safety, the observed levels at Ugali Tamu and Maziwa are probably explained by the fact that, according to the case writers, "management has limited knowledge of more advanced management techniques for translating business objectives into management practices".

For the business strategy focusing on customer orientation, the observation for Mitho Chau Chau can probably be explained by its large investment in marketing to develop its brand, the success of which does not depend on workers, and its investment in technology which substitutes labour, both of which would diminish its return on investment in cooperation. The unexpected observed level of cooperation at Suddha Vanaspati can be explained by the fact that its customer satisfaction strategy depends on consultants rather than production staff and in any case has not been successful, indicating that management does not understand the important role workers play in improving customer satisfaction.

Concerning innovation, although Taja Bakery has not been very successful in developing cooperation, owing to its policy of hiring more passive young women, it has invested heavily in good conditions of work to promote worker buy-in, which is consistent with the expectation that workers play a key role in product innovation.

Overall, business strategy, linked to the firm's mission statement and appropriately implemented, had a substantial predictive value for a firm's willingness to invest in cooperation because certain strategies depend heavily on worker input and commitment. Although a firm's business strategy is heavily influenced by a combination of other factors, both external and internal, it is not determined by them; hence the relatively weak predictive value of the other factors.

## Management strategy and competency

In theory, management strategies are designed to support the business strategy of an enterprise. In practice, there is often a lack of synergy, or worse, a conflict (see box 13).

The professionalization of human resources management often has a positive effect on the development of cooperation in an enterprise. Human resources officers who are professionally trained can apply more advanced management practices that promote transparency, consistency, predictability and fairness. These attributes help to build worker trust and confidence in management; this in turn establishes a more solid basis for trust between workers and managers. Several firms had dedicated human resources officers with professional qualifications. Sumsuman Foods in particular is so

Box 13    The importance of synergizing business, production and management strategies

The following two companies from the same country provide an interesting contrast in approach to operationalizing a business strategy.

Suddha Vanaspati demonstrates what happens when there are gaps between a firm's business, production and management strategies. Suddha Vanaspati competes on quality. It maintains and controls for quality by using advanced technology, monitoring customer satisfaction through customer surveys, safeguarding customer interests, and emphasizing workers' health and safety. At the same time, the company has shifted from export to India to expanding its share of the domestic market in Nepal. Following the loss of market share in India, management developed a "build to store" production strategy of periodically mass producing batches of ghee and ceasing production when storage capacity is full. For this they use casual labourers who lose their jobs when production ceases, and have let go many of their regular workers. Consequently, relations with the trade union have further deteriorated, and doubts exist about the firm's ability to retain high quality standards and to compete effectively – the firm's stock is trading a third below face value.

After losing its monopoly position, Shikhar Maida also decided to focus on ensuring high quality as a primary business strategy. It does this through an elaborate system which controls for quality at the critical points in the production process. This system requires close cooperation between workers and management, as worker participation is key to the success of the system. Seventy-five per cent of workers at Shikhar Maida have permanent positions, and the firm has committed to working more closely with the trade union. It has also reoriented its conditions of work and remuneration towards encouraging more worker participation. Although the firm's financial position is weaker than it was under a monopoly situation, it has been able to stabilize its share of a rapidly growing market.

committed to professionalization of its human resources staff that it has implemented a programme of continuous training and development. In general, there was a correspondence between the amount of resources invested in building the capacity of human resources staff and the level of cooperation.

However, professionalization does not guarantee an improvement in labour–management relations. Mitho Chau Chau is managed by an industrial group which presumably was chosen by the owners for its management competencies; nonetheless it has had very limited success in building cooperation between workers and managers. And, conversely, Tebe Mills and Twikki Meat have high and medium levels of cooperation respectively, despite the limited specialized training their human resources officers received.

Of course, cooperation implies a relationship where both managers and workers have a responsibility to invest. It is therefore no coincidence that the firms which have been most successful in developing cooperation also have invested the most in building the competencies of workers as well as managers. Sumsuman Foods and Dagatyaman Seafood in particular have made substantial investments in the leadership and team-building skills of workers as well as managers.

## Conclusion

A wide range of external and internal factors influence management's decision to invest in developing cooperation. External factors over which the entrepreneur has relatively little control include market structure, regulation, conditions for market access, and political climate. Although no one factor conclusively determines the extent of labour–management cooperation in an enterprise, and various factors in combination may have conflicting influences, these factors often strongly colour management's view of the importance of cooperation, and whether it is an "affordable" investment (see figure 3).

These factors influence but do not determine the level of cooperation. It is up to management ultimately to decide how to respond to them. Overall, business strategy, in particular how essential workers are in succeeding in the chosen strategy, appears to be a very strong predictor of management's willingness to invest in building cooperation (see box 14 for a comparison of two firms).

Of course, the effectiveness of cooperation in promoting a particular business strategy will depend on how well management is able to build that strategy on a framework of labour–management cooperation (see box 15 for an example).

Figure 3    Factors influencing labour–management cooperation in SMEs

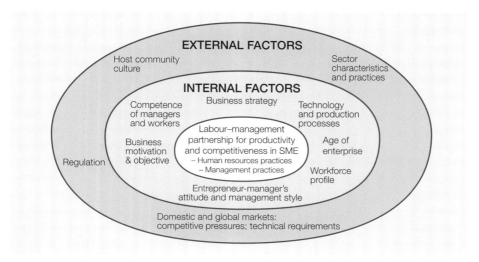

Box 14    A closer look at some forces affecting management strategies: Two firms in Botswana

A closer look at two firms in Botswana, which share a similar community culture, provide some insights into the factors shaping labour–management cooperation.

Tebe Mills was founded in 1992 by a mother and daughter. The daughter is a professionally trained nutritionist who was motivated for several reasons to become an entrepreneur:

• she desired to return her country to being self-reliant for staple foods;

• she felt it would be satisfying to establish an enterprise and to see it grow and meet the needs of the population; and

• she wanted to modernize and enrich staple foods for the benefit of the population.

The initial capitalization for the firm was P250,000 in 1992. Forty per cent of the money came from the owners, and 60 per cent from the Botswana Development Corporation in the form of grants and low interest loans. In 2003 the firm was valued at P1.5 million. The business expanded production from 120 tons per year in 1992 to 10,000 tons per year in 2003.

The key business strategy of Tebe Mills is to:

• expand production to other staple foods;

• diversify into animal feed to make use of waste material from the production process; and

• continuously improve the nutritional quality of products to create and maintain market niches.

The strong community orientation in the entrepreneur's motivation, relatively limited risk of exposure due to government subsidies, and business strategy which relies on innovation all have strongly influenced the entrepreneur's desire to develop labour–management cooperation. The management philosophy is to provide direction and empower staff:

• The job of management is to provide equipment, set standards and goals, and appraise and reward performance.

• Supervisors are responsible for production decisions independent of top management.

• And workers are empowered as they deem fit to organize production to meet the quotas and standards and to take corrective action, either in consultation with their supervisor or independently.

Twikki Meat, an abattoir, shares some of these characteristics due to a shared cultural background and similar exposure to risk, but differences in management exist because of differences in both the motivation of the founders and the business strategies.

Twikki is owned by a husband and wife, and their son helps to manage it. The husband wanted to establish a business:

- to be the boss;

- to not be forced to retire at a certain age;

- to build up assets to leave to the family; and

- to provide employment locally.

The owners put up 25 per cent of the initial capital, with the Botswana Development Corporation providing the rest in grants and loans. The enterprise was valued at P600,000 in 2003.

The business strategy aims:

- to be known for excellence, hygiene and quality of products and related services;

- to focus on market segmentation rather than expansion, in order to retain control over production processes; and

- to retain a strong customer orientation to build loyalty, including tracing orders, conducting customer surveys and quickly following up any complaints.

The management philosophy at Twikki is authoritarian concerning hygiene standards, since that is its market niche. But management aims to promote a sense of ownership and loyalty to the company among its employees. It views as essential a strong role of workers in operational decision-making, and emphasizes the importance of consultation to promote ownership of decisions by all. Management emphasizes less the position of the employee and more his or her contribution to the enterprise.

At Twikki, the entrepreneur's main motivation to be the boss, coupled with a focus on quality control rather than innovation, have pulled management towards more controlling strategies than those at Tebe Mills. At the same time, Twikki and Tebe share cultural roots in the *kgotla* system where social relations that minimize inequalities of status, similar degrees of exposure to financial risk, and similar needs to engage workers to ensure that quality is consistently high have all pushed Twikki to balance controlling strategies with management practices that more actively engage workers in the production process.

Box 15     An integrated approach to human resources management, cooperation and competitiveness

Sumsuman Foods provides a good example of a conscious effort by management to link human resources management to improving communication and cooperation, and ultimately productivity and competitiveness. Management has set itself the goal of creating a performance culture.

In the area of production management, it has implemented TQM, Quality Improvement Project, Balanced Score Card Framework, and a total customer orientation system.

These systems were put into operation in consultation with workers to gain their buy-in. Management also invests in building the knowledge base and confidence by putting in place a Continuous Education Program for all levels, including management, and a job enrichment programme. And it has implemented a complementary recruitment and selection system. Workers' confidence and skills base is further supported and expanded through job rotations which allow them to express their preferences, and open up future career development prospects.

In order to build social capital to make the productivity and human resources management systems function optimally, management sought employees' views of the organization as a whole and management's performance, and workers' views concerning production, conditions of work, benefits and so on. The information gained from this listening exercise served as the basis for improving the pay and benefits package, which was brought more closely into line with workers' needs and interests. This listening exercise, together with the improvements in pay and benefits, brought about a turnaround in employee commitment and willingness to participate in the productivity improvement programmes.

The programmes are further supported by various communication mechanisms which provide extensive direct interaction between workers and managers at all levels. These include weekly and monthly meetings, quarterly thematic discussions, and other ad hoc meetings as either workers or management deem necessary. These mechanisms also serve to channel vital information for productivity improvement.

The process of building social capital is further supported by various social interactions, including shared worship services, annual picnics and retreats surrounding religious holidays, and a monthly newsletter to which both management and workers contribute.

The higher level of trust in the enterprise resulting from these efforts enables management to emphasize, and workers to accept, higher levels of responsibility and accountability, which are supported in turn by incentive-based compensation and performance-based pay. This "blurring of lines between workers and managers" creates a more agile and responsive enterprise.

# CONCLUSION

# 6

This study has argued that labour–management cooperation is the key to creating a virtuous circle between productivity and decent work in an enterprise. Cooperation involves shared goals, efforts, and information. It also facilitates learning, which encourages innovation, flexibility and more effective change management. Hence, cooperation is essential to improve productivity and competitiveness.

The analysis of the forms of cooperation that exist in the cases studied indicate that:

- Management in three firms was unwilling to invest in cooperation and preferred either to substitute more advanced technology for labour, or to buy worker compliance through higher benefits and better conditions of work.

- In three cases, the low level of investment was probably due not to unwillingness but to limited capability.

- In the remaining cases, management was committed to developing cooperation and made moderate to extensive investments to this end.

The cases indicate that management in the majority of firms made a conscious effort to put in place policies and practices that motivate workers to contribute to enterprise performance. Most managers identified a link between conditions of work, training and development, safety and health, and good labour–management relations on the one hand, and cooperation and partnership on the other, as important means for improving enterprise productivity and competitiveness.

However, the scope and mechanisms for achieving the objective of pro-productivity human resources polices varied from one firm to another. This was due in part to differences in pressure from product market specifications and intensity of competition, and to the differing impacts of these pressures. While certification standards for market access served to encourage firms to develop more formal, transparent and participatory human resources policies geared towards productivity improvement, market and competitive pressures had a more mixed effect. In some cases, the pressure motivated firms to upgrade their human resources systems; but in others such pressure created a disincentive to change, for fear of increasing the firm's exposure to risk.

Lax enforcement of labour legislation also acted as a disincentive to modernize human resources practices in certain areas, such as occupational health and safety; and some of the cases demonstrate how more effective enforcement of labour legislation can spur firms to upgrade their human resources systems.

Nonetheless, even those firms with relatively structured and advanced human resources systems considered it essential to maintain flexibility and some degree of informality in their human resources management strategies and systems, to enable these small firms to respond quickly to their changing environment. Flexibility and informality can serve simply as an excuse for unilateral decision-making that does not take into account the needs, concerns or ideas of workers. Indeed, that appeared to be the case to some degree in a few of the firms studied. In other cases, however, management appeared to take into consideration workers' preferences, or to compensate for unilateral decision-making with welfare programmes that went beyond the requirements of the law, with the aim of strengthening the bond of trust and commitment between the workers and owners to enhance productivity. And some firms demonstrated an awareness of the negative effect informality and flexibility can have on the growth of the firm.

In addition, the desire for a less formal approach to human resources management stemmed from many entrepreneurs' desire to create a familial atmosphere in the workplace, which often meant managing with a mix of paternalism and benevolence. It also stemmed in part from the deep roots the firms all had in the local community, which added a broader context to the employment relationship that helped to discourage abusive management practices, and helped to compensate for the lack of safeguards and relative security that a more formal system can provide to workers.

A further reason for the continued survival of informality is that most SMEs are not usually members of industry employers' associations, or are only marginally associated with them. As a result they are not necessarily bound by an industry agreement, leaving them with considerable leeway to determine their human resources management and employment relations policies. Even in Kenya, where two of the small firms apply the sectoral agreement, this is done selectively and is limited to wages, as the firms find it difficult to operate within the rules of such agreements which are often more suited to larger firms. Nonetheless, formalization tends to increase over time, as human resources management becomes more specialized.

A number of factors explain the rate of unionization among the small firms studied. The readiness of government to enforce statutory protections for the right to organize is an important factor influencing whether management accepts or resists having a union. In Nepal and Kenya, where public policy support for unionism is unequivocal, there is a much higher rate of union activity in small enterprises. In contrast, the laissez-faire approach prevalent in Botswana and the Philippines has resulted in a lower rate of organized workers in SMEs. As a result the tendency is for small firms to adopt other forms of management. At one end of the spectrum of such options is paternalism or benevolence, with autocracy and authoritarianism at the other end. The nature of the small firms makes the development of any of these forms feasible with relative ease. As the cases show, trade unions have not undertaken a determined and aggressive unionization of workers in most of the small firms, due to limited staff and resources, and a tendency to prioritize the organization of workers in larger firms.

However, recognition of a union does not guarantee that management and worker representatives will work together. This is partly due to management attitudes impeding cooperation on the one hand, and the often limited capacity and experience of the workers' representatives on the other. When the shop steward structure was weak or non-existent, management interaction with the union was minimal, reinforcing negative attitudes towards unions as weak and ineffective and providing management with an excuse for not working with them. This was particularly so in Kenya where much of trade union activity concerned no more than the implementation of the sectoral wage agreement; hence the legitimacy of the union in the firms was less established.

The willingness of firms to invest in cooperation is shaped by a range of internal and external factors, which are continuously changing. Overall, business strategy appears to be a very strong predictor of management's willingness to invest in building cooperation. Business strategy is the choice of management, albeit influenced to varying degrees by the other factors which are themselves changing and continuously reshaping the business strategy. Hence, it would appear that deterministic models that assert that certain factors such as market structure or regulation make it difficult or impossible for small firms to invest in building cooperation are limited in their predictive value.

Although one case demonstrated that it is possible for a small enterprise to compete effectively, at least in the short term, without developing cooperation, the vast majority of cases studied indicate, either positively or by counter-example, that labour–management cooperation is important to successful performance in competitive markets, at least in the food processing sub-sector. Managers who are interested in improving their competitive position should consider ways of developing effective communication channels and means of cooperating. Policy-makers and institutions supporting small enterprises should consider means of raising the awareness of the importance of labour–management cooperation, and of helping managers and workers in small firms to develop their capacity to do so.

# ENTERPRISES STUDIED

**Dagatyaman Seafood, Inc.** is a marine product processing company located in Cordova, Philippines. It was established in 1999 by an entrepreneur with initial capital of 2 million pesos. Dagatyaman is heavily export-oriented, with 90 per cent of its products shipped to the United States market, and is HACCP certified. The company aims to provide the most reasonably priced, globally accepted quality seafood products anywhere in the market. Annual sales averages 10 million US dollars per year, and the company has demonstrated consistently impressive financial performance.

Dagatyaman employs 50 regular employees and 150 seasonal workers during the peak months of August to December. Most workers are recruited locally. Eighty per cent of all the CSI workers are women, mostly in their 20s. Workers are paid above the minimum wage, between P210 and P240 per day, depending on experience; but seasonal workers receive less than the minimum wage. Regular employees also receive statutory benefits such as social security coverage; five days paid leave, five days paid sick leave, and five days service incentive leave per year; two months paid maternity leave for women; and 13th month salary. They also receive life insurance (75 per cent of the premium paid by the company), and mid-year and year-end productivity bonuses. Training is provided through rotated shift assignments on a weekly basis. Among the activities conducted are leadership, supervisory management, teambuilding courses (the same courses are given to the suppliers considered as stakeholders to organize and contribute to the capacity building of its suppliers. Workers are also encouraged to undergo training activities offered by other institutions such as the University of the Philippines School of Labour and Industrial Relations.

There are four levels of decision-making: company president, shift supervisors, section leaders and workers, who are also empowered to make decisions. Management recognizes the need to provide a more formal channel for employee participation in productivity improvement and continuous product development and innovation. The company is not unionized, but management does not express any hostility to worker organization.

**Masapat Farms, Inc.,** a family-owned and operated enterprise established in 1984, is located in Angeles City and Barangay Duquit Mabalacat, Philippines. It originally produced cassava meals for feeding livestock, and charcoal, and diversified in 1989 into cattle breeding and in 1999 into meat products such as hotdogs and smoked meats. Masapat focuses exclusively on the domestic market, but aims to expand to exports once its domestic market position is secure. The company competes on quality and has received several awards. It has experienced high growth of sales in recent years, e.g., in 2002 sales increased 30 per cent.

As of 2003 Masapat employed 152 workers, 66 per cent of whom have regular contracts, 5 per cent are on probation, and 29 per cent are casual workers. Eighty per cent of the workforce are young males in their 20s, and the hiring policy specifies that new recruits must not be over 24 years old and must be single. Women workers are assigned to do office work in the administrative office, human resources section, finance and marketing. Workers are recruited on referral from relatives or current regular employees, and priority in hiring is given to applicants living within the local community.

The company pays workers according to skills, experience and responsibilities, and respects the law concerning the minimum wage and overtime compensation for all workers. Workers with more experience and skills are paid more. Workers, including seasonal workers, are entitled to become a member of the cooperative which pays members a dividend at the end of the year. Regular contract workers also receive a 13th month salary, Christmas gifts, coverage in health and retirement plans, paid sick and vacation leave and discounts on products. Training focuses on safety and productivity.

The company is not organized. Management is not in favour of a union and discourages organizing by granting benefits and assistance to employees in part to avoid workers organizing. As part of this strategy management involves workers in designing an incentive scheme for productivity improvement which includes productivity incentives for each section, computing daily outputs, cash awards to individuals and teams, and a penalty system for wastage, poor performance, or misconduct.

**Maziwa Limited** is a family-owned and operated dairy established in 1996 which produces milk, yoghurt, butter, ghee, and cream under different brand names for various market segments (hotels, hospitals, schools, supermarkets, other retail outlets, and export to the European Union). It is located in the Githunguri area of Kiambu District in Central Province of Kenya, and has grown from an initial capitalization of Ksh. 5 million in 1996 to Ksh. 8.4 million in 2002, with annual revenues of Ksh. 28 million. The company follows an aggressive marketing and low-price strategy, with product differentiation, intensified promotional activities, and development and expansion of distribution systems and linkages.

The number of employees has grown from three in 1996 to 26 permanent and 23 casual workers in 2003. Twenty-seven per cent of the permanent staff are women. The management is professionally trained, with three levels of decision-making. Workers are not involved in decision-making. New employees receive the statutory minimum wage, which allows for different wage rates depending on employee skill level and the geographical location of the firm. More senior workers are paid higher rates set at the discretion of the management who uses profitability as the criteria for determination. Workers are also entitled to medical services, maternity leave, house allowances, and 21 days (paid as one month) of annual leave for all employees. Training is sporadic.

Maziwa was unionized initially, but the workers voted to withdraw, viewing the union as too weak to provide effective representation on grievance and negotiation. Management expressed a negative perception of union management as anti-productivity and infringing on their right to manage. There is no collective bargaining or significant consultation.

**Mchuzi Safi Limited** is located in the industrial district in Nairobi, Kenya. It was established in 1975 with initial capital of Ksh. 2 million, and is owned and operated by three brothers. The company produces spices, herbs, groundnuts and crisps for local supermarkets, restaurants, and hotels, as well as exporting to the United Republic of Tanzania, Uganda and and the United States. Sales turnover has grown from Ksh. 61.2 million in 1998 to 86.1 million in 2002, due in part to growth of its product lines and commitment to quality. It plans to expand to other foreign markets in the region, but in the context of a controlled growth strategy.

Mchuzi Safi employs 90 workers on a permanent basis (61 per cent are female), and relatively few seasonal workers for the industry. There are three levels of decision-making, but no formal organizational structures. Workers are recruited widely, but promotion to line and functional management positions are made from among the employees with sales and customer contact experience. Training programmes are concentrated on staff in sales positions, with little provided on productivity upgrading.

Workers in the company are organized but the relationship between management and the union representatives is acrimonious, with many disputes ending up in the industrial courts. Collective bargaining generally exists only for the goals that coincide with goals set by management. Workers are paid substantially above the minimum rate required by law, but in response to the decision to organize, management eliminated the 5–8 per cent increase per year (depending on business performance) it had traditionally granted. Other benefits include: health, accident, disability, and life insurance; savings and pension plans; and paid vacation (25–27 days, depending on length of service). The turnover rate is low for the sector, in part because of the firm's belief in permanent employment and minimal use of temporary workers.

Mchuzi Safi lacks a realistic and systematic productivity improvement strategy. However, it aims to enhance product quality through creation of strong backward linkages with its suppliers. There is little labour–management partnership. Managers at all levels are empowered to take decisions and be "entrepreneurially creative" but workers are not authorized to take any decisions and no participatory processes exist for consultation.

**Mitho Chau Chau Ltd.** is located in Sunsari, Nepal and produces instant noodles and other snack foods. It was established in 2000 with a family investment of Rs. 130 million, and is professionally managed. The firm produces principally for the domestic market, but exports about 15 per cent of its product; and it is currently expanding its share of the domestic market, with a focus on quality at a low price. Sales have grown from 4,725 metric tons in 1993 to 13,845 metric tons in 2001.

Mitho Chau Chau has 170 regular staff, 10 of whom have permanent status; and up to 300 non-regular workers who are hired when necessary, depending on the level of production.

There are 50 female workers in the company, of whom three have permanent positions.

Three levels of management exist, with no decision-making power given to workers. Workers are hired locally. The age limit for hiring is 35 years and the recruit must be a Nepalese citizen. Regular workers are paid the statutory minimum wage, overtime premium and paid public holidays, and are covered by a provident fund. Other workers are paid the minimum wage only. Some training programmes exist.

There are two unions in the company, neither of which is recognized because no election has taken place. Nonetheless, a committee for collective bargaining has been established, with five members from each of the two trade unions. As a result of collective bargaining, the workers have secured some facilities and benefits (public holidays, remuneration in lieu of accumulated leaves, 50 per cent of sick leave to be paid in cash, 10 per cent provident fund facility to the permanent workers, festival allowance to permanent workers, night allowance of Rs. 3, life and accident insurance as stipulated in the Labour Act, four days of paid leave per year to the authorized union members to perform union duties, a free medical check-up for all workers, 10 per cent bonus distribution after five years of company profit, a bicycle stand facility, a dress allowance). The unions are not given a role in productivity improvement.

**Shikhar Maida Ltd** is located in Hatenda Industrial district in Makwanpur, Nepal. It was established in 1970, and became a publicly held company in 1992. Shikhar Maida produces wheat products, including flour and bran, mainly for the domestic market, but some is exported to Tibet. Shikhar is the first modern mill in Nepal, and enjoyed a near monopoly position for a long time until the establishment of 22 new flourmills eroded its market dominance. The mill is still running at a profit, but the margin has dwindled sharply. The company aims to stay competitive through closely controlling quality, cutting costs and becoming more flexible.

Shikhar employs a total of 80 workers. Sixty-one workers, of whom three are women, have permanent positions. The company pays workers based on their skills level and experience, with all workers receiving at least the minimum wage. Other benefits include: housing allowance, medical allowance, education allowance for up to two children; and salary advances can be obtained to buy a bicycle or purchase land. An employee welfare committee exists, with equal representation of management and workers; however, the need to cut costs has weakened the union's bargaining position on benefits. The firm has invested in skills development at all levels, focused on productivity improvement schemes such as 5S and cleaner production.

There are three levels of decision-making: a board of directors, a general manager, and production managers, with consultation with union representatives. In general, management and union representatives state that they aim for a cooperative approach to decision-making and management. This has resulted in no strikes in the mill since 1982, which is unusual for the sector, and in management–union agreement to a voluntary retirement system instead of retrenchments to reduce the labour force. Management reports that participation in training programmes has helped to motivate workers.

**Suddha Vanaspati Ltd.** is located in Sunsari, Nepal near the border with India. It is a publicly held company established in 1992 by two holding companies, and is professionally managed. It produces vegetable ghee, most of which is exported to India; but the company aims to develop a stronger presence in the domestic market. The company currently is running at a loss, due to import restrictions limiting access to the Indian market, and intense competition in the domestic market.

The company employs 85 people as permanent staff, and in addition a large number of daily wage earners (between 100 and 200, depending on the production level). There are only two female employees among the permanent staff. The firm recruits mostly foreign workers from India, in order to "neutralize the trade union's activity". All workers are paid the statutory minimum wage, with more paid according to length of service. Benefits provided to permanent workers include: accident insurance, clothing, shoes, Dasai festival allowance, medical check-ups, overtime payments, five per cent annual grade increment, payment even at time of factory closure and 10 per cent bonus as laid down by the Nepal Bonus Act. Workers are generally illiterate, and are provided with only basic on-the-job training.

There are six levels of managerial decision-making, with no worker involvement or consultation. An authorized trade union exists, which is affiliated with a national trade union confederation. This union replaced the pre-existing trade union, all the members of which were fired from the company. Management is still hostile to unions, describing the new union as a problem-creating group of workers more controlled by external politics than by the internal needs of the workers; and the trade unions for their part do not believe the firm's accounts showing huge losses are accurate. The union meets only off site and collective bargaining is restricted to the issues specified in law.

**Sumsuman Foods, Inc.** is a family-owned producer of snack foods made from pork and chicken skin (*chicharron*), vinegar and dried fruits. It was established in 2001 with an initial capitalization of 12 million pesos and is located in Cebu, Philippines. Sumsuman dominates the high end of the domestic market for chicharron, competing on quality, packaging, and innovation; and aims to expand exports. Product sales surged in 2002 but declined in 2003 and have since levelled, but the company continues to stay robust and profitable, in part due to aggressive cost-cutting measures and low overheads. It was voted the "Best meat establishment in 2001–2002".

Sumsuman employs 50 workers (referred to as "associates"), 70 per cent of whom are male. Management is young (in their early 30s) and professionally trained. Recruitment is done through referrals by existing employees. Workers are paid at least the statutory minimum, with salary increases tied to performance (both individual and collective). Workers also receive overtime pay, night differential premium, payment for work on holidays, and performance bonuses of 8–10 per cent of the company's net earnings. Management actively seeks input from individual workers and production teams, through awards and other recognition schemes, for improving: products or service quantity and quality through rationalization of work hours, careful inspection of own work, zero waste, optimum utilization of materials, product quality improvements, improvements in the packaging quality design and production; health and safety; and management efficiency.

Managers and department heads are evaluated using the 360-degree feedback method; and once a year each associate participates in a one-on-one talk on any work-related topic or more general concerns with the president. Management has invested substantially in workers' training programmes since it is been in the process of becoming certified as a Hazard Analysis and Critical Control Point (HACCP); it adheres to good manufacturing practices (GMP) and good sanitation practices (GSP); and practises job rotation activities where associates are placed in areas or stations that interest them.

Management follows a non-interference policy concerning freedom of association. Sumsuman employees are not organized into a union. The company's strong emphasis on religion (sponsoring Bible study sessions, arranging for staff to attend Mass together on holidays, religious outings) may have some impact on the workers' decision, but there is no clear evidence for this.

**Taja Bakery** is a family-owned and managed enterprise located South of Lalitpur District in Kathmandou Valley, Nepal. It was established in 1994 with an investment of Rs. 10 million, and produces bread, cookies and puff pastries. The enterprise has grown from working out of a home to 30 bakeries. Taja now has approximately 20 per cent of the market share. It aims to be the leader in the bakery industry, and consequently has introduced more advanced technology, cost and quality control mechanisms, and human resources management.

Taja Bakery currently employs 276 workers. It hires exclusively young women for production, most of whom are not married. Management organization is changing from an informal to a formal system, but there is no formal organizational structure yet and decision-making is still divided among family members. Informal channels are used for recruiting workers through relatives and friends. Workers are paid at least the minimum wage prescribed by the government and salaries vary between Rs. 1,800–3,500. Sales staff also receive a five per cent commission on sales. Other benefits include dormitories for night-workers, overtime allowance, first aid services, lunch and dinner provided for each shift, dress allowance, paid festival leave, and attendance bonuses. Management plans to introduce a health insurance package and a saving account. Training provided includes: literacy classes, training on 5S, and information provided on HIV/AIDS. The company also is contemplating a career development plan for workers so that each worker after leaving the company can be more independent financially.

There is no authorized union in the company. Management does not feel it necessary to have a union in the company because it believes that it can fulfil the role of a union through daily staff meetings with workers. But line managers often complain of staff non-cooperation. At the end of the month, the managing director attends the meeting and examines personal problems of the staff regarding salary and other matters related to work.

**Tebe Mills** is owned and managed by a mother and daughter. It is located in a rural area 40 kilometres north of Gaborone, Botswana and produces sorghum. It was established in 1992, with 250,000 pula; total assets reached P1.5 million in 2003 while annual turnover was P17.3 million. The firm produces for the domestic market, and market share has grown rapidly. The firm's key productivity objectives are to diversify into products which can make use of the waste from the milled sorghum, and to improve quality. Both strategies were proposed by the workers and they play a key role, particularly in quality improvement.

The workforce has grown from eight employees in 1992 to 120 working three shifts in 2003. 81 per cent of its workers are permanent; and 49.5 per cent are women. Workers are recruited locally and promoted from within. The company has a lean organizational structure characterized by four levels of decision-making, although line workers are authorized to make many operational decisions themselves. The management philosophy is to generate loyalty, build trust, and promote a sense of belonging among employees, in part by delegating significant decision-making authority to them. Workers receive the statutory minimum wage together with a bonus based on individual performance. Other benefits include: support for establishing micro-enterprises, shower facilities and use of the telephone. Training is limited to the basic skills needed, but is made available to all workers. Performance appraisals are 360-degree.

There is no union, but informal associations exist by operation function, to enable workers to discuss problems and concerns collectively with management, and to jointly set quotas and quality standards and take corrective actions in case of deviation. Consultations involving the entire workforce take place in the *kyotla* system (traditional meeting place for a community). The turnover rate is average, with 70 per cent having spent less than three years with the company.

**Twikki Meat** was established in 1970 in southern Botwana. It was subsequently bought by a family which still manages it. Twikki produces quality processed and fresh halal meat for retail and bulk customers, with a system of just-in-time production and delivery. Annual turnover has grown from P250,000 in 1994 to P600,000 in 2003. The firm aims to sell nationally and raise the turnover to between P700,000–800,000.

Staff size has grown from 32 employees in 1994 to 65 employees in 2003. Currently 48 per cent of workers are women. There are four levels of decision-making. Workers are recruited locally, primarily based on referrals from existing employees. Twikki pays all workers at least the statutory minimum for the sector and region (P500) up to P4,500 for senior staff. Other benefits provided include: use of shower facilities, discounts on company products purchased, two hot meals per shift, life insurance and funeral insurance for worker and relatives, and a retirement welfare fund. The firm does not invest in training courses because the high rate of poaching among competitors and the important role of the industry in the economy has motivated the government to provide free training.

The management style is based on a structure with a lot of informality and there is an involvement of the workers in the operational decisions of the company, through regular meetings held, a consultative and participative management (labour–management meetings held monthly and unscheduled ones for top management). Managers and production staff together plan production and schedules and decide how much overtime is to be allocated to each worker. For issues concerning the entire workforce, the *kgotla* system is used for dialogue and consultation. The company is not unionized. The turnover rate is low for the industry, and 10 employees have been with the company since 1994.

**Ugali Tamu Ltd,** located in Nairobi, Kenya, was established in 1967 with Ksh. 100,000. As of 2003 the firm was valued at Ksh. 50 million. It is owned and managed by a family and packages grains and cereals for the wholesale and retail markets in Kenya, Canada, India and the United States. The firm is growing fast, due to exports, but wants to shift focus to expanding its share of the local market. Sales have steadily declined from Ksh. 216.5 million in 1998 to 64.8 million in 2002, due to unfavourable production and trading conditions.

The workforce has grown from nine employees in 1967 to 20 permanent and 24 casual workers in 2003. Of the permanent workers, three are women. The firm has a policy of hiring young and energetic workers, and promotes from within to the levels of line and middle management. Workers are paid at least the minimum wage, with higher wages paid to more highly skilled workers. Workers also receive: a housing allowance which varies with their position and years of service; 27 days of paid annual leave; maternity leave; savings and pensions plans; medical services through the company doctor; and accident, disability, and life insurance. Management provides on-the-job training in the areas of operations and accounting, and external training for marketing, computing and other management development programmes.

Rapid changes and business expansion have necessitated the adoption of a new organizational structure and leadership. Management established a participatory framework to promote problem solving, decision-making, employee ownership plans, productivity management, staff unionization, human resources development, wages and other terms and conditions of employment. Nonetheless, the company still lacks a participatory approach to developing performance management techniques, tools and review programmes. The company aspires to provide a broad range of quality and affordable processed food products to the Kenyan and regional market; improve production and quality control practices; increase international sales and profitability; and increase sales earnings and earnings per share by 15 per cent per year and achieve a 20 per cent return on equity. Workers are entitled to be represented by the Kenya Union of Commercial, Food and Allied Workers, but have not organized.

## Profiles of enterprises: A summary

| Company name | Year established | Ownership structure | Men/ Women | Permanent/ non-permanent/ seasonal | Union/ management hostility to union | Products | Market | Human resources strategies | Business strategies |
|---|---|---|---|---|---|---|---|---|---|
| **Philippines** | | | | | | | | | |
| Dagatyaman Seafoods | 1999 | Incorporated Individual | 40/160 | 50/150 | No/no | Seafoods | 90 per cent export | • Good conditions of work<br>• High investment in training<br>• Workers empowered to make decisions | • HACCP<br>• Strong customer orientation<br>• Strong brand |
| Masapat Farms | 1984 | Incorporated Family | 112/40 | 100/52 | No/some | Meat products | Domestic | • Higher wages and benefits to discourage unionization<br>• Worker participation schemes | • Product diversity<br>• Market expansion |
| Sumsuman Foods | 2001 | Incorporated Family | 35/15 | 50/0 | No/no | Chicharon | 15 per cent export | • Good conditions of work<br>• High investment in training<br>• Encourages participation in religious activities | • Costcutting<br>• Working towards HACCP |
| **Nepal** | | | | | | | | | |
| Mitho Chau Chau | 2000 | Incorporated Family | 120/50 | 10/160/300 | Two unions, not recognized but able to bargain collectively | Instant noodles | 15 per cent export | • Minimum legally required pay and benefits<br>• Minimal investment in training<br>• Worker initiative not encouraged | • Aggressive market expansion<br>• Strong customer orientation |

/cont'd.

Profiles of enterprises: A summary *(cont'd)*

/cont'd.

| Company name | Year established | Ownership structure | Men/ Women | Permanent/ non-permanent/ seasonal | Union/ management hostility to union | Products | Market | Human resources strategies | Business strategies |
|---|---|---|---|---|---|---|---|---|---|
| **Nepal** *(/cont'd)* | | | | | | | | | |
| Shikhar Maida | 1970 | Publicly held | 77/3 | 61/20 | Yes/no | Flour and bran | Domestic | • Very good conditions of work<br>• Strong cooperation with union<br>• High investment in skills development | • High quality<br>• Cut non-labour costs<br>• Operate more flexibly |
| Suddha Vanaspati | 1992 | Publicly held | 83/2 | 85/100 | Yes/yes | Ghee | Domestic<br><br>Export to India | • Minimum legally required pay and benefits<br>• Minimal investment in training<br>• Hostile to union<br>• Relies heavily on temporary workers<br>• Recruits foreign workers o weaken union | • High quality<br>• Export<br>• Produce large quantities periodically to store |
| Taja Bakery | 1994 | Incorporated Family | 136/140 | 276 | No/hires "docile" young women to avoid unionization | Bread and cookies | Domestic | • Good wages and benefits<br>• Informal management structure<br>• Encourages worker communication and participation | • Low cost, high quality<br>• Aggressive expansion<br>• Upgrade technology |

| | | | | | | | | | |
|---|---|---|---|---|---|---|---|---|---|
| **Kenya** | | | | | | | | | |
| Maziwa | 1996 | Incorporated Family | 19/7 | 26/23 | No (workers withdrew)/yes | Dairy products, ghee | Domestic Some export to EU | • Statutory pay and allowances<br>• Limited training<br>• Limited communication or consultation | • Aggressive marketing<br>• Low cost<br>• Product differentiation and market segmentation<br>• Strong distribution channels |
| Mchuzi Safi | 1975 | Limited company Family | 39/51 | 90 | Yes/yes | Spices, herbs and nuts | Export Domestic | • Statutory minimum pay and benefits<br>• Training concentrated on sales staff | • Aggressive marketing<br>• Aims to improve quality and productivity, but no actual strategy |
| Ugali Tamu | 1967 | Limited company Family | 17/3 | 20/24 | No/no | Grains and Cereals | Export Domestic | • Good benefits<br>• Investment in worker nd management training<br>• Worker communication nd participation encouraged, but management capacity for cooperation limited | • Aggressive marketing<br>• Decreased dependence on exports |
| **Botswana** | | | | | | | | | |
| Tebe Mills | 1992 | Incorporated Mother and daughter | 60/60 | 120 | No/no | Sorghum | Local domestic market | • Good working conditions<br>• Rapid growth of staff<br>• Empowers workers to take initiatives<br>• Factory-wide consultations | • Product diversification to minimize waste<br>• Cost non-labour costs<br>• Improve productivity and quality |

/cont'd.

115

## Profiles of enterprises: A summary *(cont'd)*

| Company name | Year established | Ownership structure | Men/ Women | Permanent/ non-permanent/ seasonal | Union/ management hostility to union | Products | Market | Human resources strategies | Business strategies |
|---|---|---|---|---|---|---|---|---|---|
| **Botswana** *(cont'd)* | | | | | | | | | |
| Twikki Meat | 1970 | Incorporated Family | 34/31 | 65 | No | Processed halal meat | Local domestic market | • Good working conditions<br>• Informal management<br>• Wide consultation<br>• Worker participation encouraged | • Quality<br>• Just-in-time production<br>• Rapid delivery<br>• Diversified customer base |

# BIBLIOGRAPHY

Abbott, B. 1993. "Small firms and trade unions in services in the 1990s", in *Industrial Relations Journal*, Vol. 24, No. 4, pp. 308–317.

Atkinson, J. B.; Storey, D. (eds.). 1994. *Employment, the small firm and the labour market* (London, Routledge).

Bacon, N.; Ackers, P.; Storey, J; Coates, D. 1996. "It's a small world: Managing human resources in small businesses", in *International Journal of Human Resource Management*, Vol. 7, No. 1, pp. 82–100.

Beaumont, P. (ed.). 1995. *The future of employment relations* (London, Sage).

*Bolton Report, The*. 1971. Report of the Committee of Inquiry on Small Firms. Cmnd.4811 (London, HMSO).

Boselie, J. P.; Jansen, P. 2001. "Human resource management and performance: lessons from the Netherlands", in *International Journal of Human Resource Management*, Vol. 12, No. 7, pp. 1107–1125.

Boxall, P. 1996. "The strategic HRM debate and the resource-based view of the firm", in *Human Resource Management Journal*, Vol. 6, No. 3, pp. 59–75.

Brown, C.; Hamilton, J; Medoff, J. 1990. *Employers large and small* (Cambridge, Mass., Harvard University Press).

Burt, R. 1996. "The social capital of entrepreneurial managers", in *Financial Times* (London), European edition, 5 May.

Capelli, P.; Crocker-Hefter, A. 1996. "Distinctive human resources are firms' core competencies", in *Organizational Dynamics*, Vol. 24, No. 3, pp 7–22.

Carroll, M.; Marchington, M.; Earnshaw, J.; Taylor, S. 1999. "Recruitment in small firms: Processes, methods and problems", in *Employee Relations*, Vol. 21, No. 3, pp. 236–250.

Coleman, J. 1988. "Social capital formation and the creation of human capital", in *American Journal of Sociology*, Vol. 94 (supplement), S95–S120.

Costa, A.C. 2003. "Work team trust and effectiveness", in *Personnel Review*, Vol. 32, No. 5, pp. 605–622.

Currant, J.; Abbolt, B.; Mills, V. 1993. *Employment and employment relations in the small service sector enterprises* (London: Centre for Research on Small Services Sector Enterprises).

Dasgupta, P. 2005. "Economics of social capital", in *The Economic Record*, Vol. 81, No. s1, pp. S2–S21.

Dirks, K. T. 1999. "The effects of interpersonal trust on work group performance", in *Journal of Applied Psychology*, No. 84, pp. 445–455.

Doeringer, P.; Evans-Klock, C.; Terkla, D. 2002. *Start-up factories: High-performance management, job quality, and regional advantage* (Oxford, Oxford University Press).

Dundon, T.; Grugulis, I.; Wilkinson, A. 1999. "Looking out of the black-hole: Non-union relations in an SME", in *Employee Relations*, Vol. 21, No. 3, pp. 251–266.

Edwards, P. K. (ed.). 1995. *Industrial relations in Britain* (Oxford, Blackwell).

Eisenhardt, K. M. 1989. "Building theories from case study research", in *Academy of Management Review*, Vol.14, No.4, pp.352–550.

European Foundation for the Improvement of Living and Working Conditions. 2001. "Employment relations in micro and small enterprises in the EU – literature review main results", available in electronic format only at http://www.eurofound.eu.int/ publications/htmlfiles/ef0286.htm

Freeman, R.; Medoff, J. 1984. *What do unions do?* (New York, Basic Books).

Ghose, A. K. 2003. *Jobs and incomes in a globalizing world* (Geneva, ILO).

Gibb, A. 1997. "Small firms' training and competitiveness: Building upon the small business as a learning organization", in *International Small Business Journal*, Vol. 15, No. 3, Apr.–Jun.

Goss, D. 1991. *Small business and society* (London, Routledge).

Guest, D. 1997. "Human resource management and performance: A review and research agenda" in *International Journal of Human Resource Management*, Vol. 8, No. 3, pp. 263–276.

—. 2001. "Human resource management: When research confronts theory", in *International Journal of Human Resource Management*, Vol. 12, No. 7, pp. 1092–1106.

—; Conway, N. 1999. "Peering into the black hole: The downside of the new employee relations in the UK", in *British Journal of Industrial Relations*, No. 37, pp. 367–389.

Horstman, B. 1999. "Decentralised and deregulated Australian industrial relations: The effects on HRM and IR in small enterprises", in *Employee Relations*, Vol. 21, No. 3, pp. 325–340.

Huselid, M. 1995. "The impact of human resource management practices on turnover, productivity and corporate financial performance", in *Academy of Management Journal*, Vol. 38, No. 3 (Jun.), pp. 635–672.

International Labour Office (ILO). 1997. *General conditions to stimulate job creation in small and medium-sized enterprises*, Report V(1), International Labour Conference, 85th Session (Geneva).

—. 1998. *Note on the proceedings*. Tripartite Meeting on Technology and Employment in the Food and Drink Industries, Geneva, 18–22 May 1998.

International Organisation for Standardisation (ISO). 2000. ISO 9000, available at www. iso.org

Jennings, P.; Beaver, G. 1997. "The performance and competitive advantage of small firms: A management perspective", in *International Small Business Journal*, Vol. 15, No. 2, pp. 63–75.

Kinnie, N.; Purcell, J; Hutchinson, S. 1999. "Employment relations in SMEs: Market-driven or customer-shaped?" in *Employee Relations*, Vol. 21, No. 3, pp. 218–235.

Kochan, T. A.; Osterman, P. 1994. *The mutual gains enterprise* (Boston, Harvard Business School Press).

Lall, S. 2002. *Social capital and industrial transformation*. Queen Elizabeth House (QEH) Working Papers Series (Oxford).

Levin, D.; Cross, R. 2004. "The strength of weak ties you can trust: The mediating role of trust in effective knowledge transfer", in *Management Science*, Vol. 50, No. 11, pp. 1477–1490.

Loan-Clarke, J.; Boocock, G.; Smith, A.; Whittaker, J. 1999. "Investment in management training and development by small businesses", in *Employee Relations*, Vol. 21, No. 3, pp. 296–310.

Marchington, M.; Grugulis, I. 2000. " 'Best practice' human resource management: Perfect opportunity or dangerous illusion?", in *International Journal of Human Resource Management*, Vol. 11, No. 6, pp. 1104–1124.

Marlow, S. 2001. "Employment relations in small and micro firms", contribution to the European Foundation for the Improvement of Living and Working Conditions (Brussels).

—; Patton, D. 2000. *Minding the gap between employers and employees : The challenge for owner-managers of smaller manufacturing firms* (Leicester, Leicestershire Centre for Enterprise).

Maskell, P. 2000. *Social capital, innovation and competitiveness*, Business Studies Working Paper 2001–2, subsequently published in S. Baron, J. Field and T. Schuller (eds.); *Social capital: A critical perspective* (Oxford, Oxford University Press).

Matlay, H. 1999. "Employee relations in small firms: A micro-business perspective", in *Employee Relations*, Vol. 21, No. 3, pp. 285–295.

Pearson, A. M.; Dutson, T. R. 2001. *HACCP in meat, poultry and fish processing* (New York, Aspen).

Rainnie, A.1989. *Industrial relations in small firms: Small isn't beautiful* (London, Routledge).

Ramaswamy, E. A.; Schiphorst, F. B. 2000. "Human resource management, trade unions and empowerment: Two cases from India," in *International Journal of Human Resource Management*, Vol. 11, No. 4, pp. 664–680.

Ritchie, J. 1993. "Strategies for human resource management: Challenges in smaller and entrepreneurial organisations", in R. Harrison (ed.): *Human resource management* (Wokingham, Addison-Wesley) pp. 111–135.

Roberts, I.; Sawbridge, D; Bamber, G. 1992. "Employee relations in smaller enterprises", in B. Towers (ed.): *Handbook of industrial relations practice* (London, Kogan Page).

Rosow, J. M.; Casner-Lotto, J. 1994. "People, partnership, and profits: The new labor-management agenda", in *Strategic Partners for High Performance* (New York, Work in America Institute), pp. 73–138.

Schuller, T. 2001. "The complementary roles of human and social capital", in *ISUMA – Canadian Journal of Policy Research*, Vol. 2, No. 1.

Schumacher, F. 1974. *Small is beautiful* (London, Abacus).

Sengenberger, W., Loveman, G. W.; Piore, M. J. (eds.). 1990. *The re-emergence of small enterprises: Industrial restructuring in industrialized countries* (Geneva, International Institute for Labour Studies).

Sisson, K. 1993. "In search of human resource management", in *British Journal of Industrial Relations*, Vol. 31, No. 2, pp. 201–210.

de Soto, H. 2000. *The mystery of capital: Why capitalism triumphs in the West and fails everywhere else* (New York, Basic Books).

Tannock, J.; Krasacholl, L.; Ruangpermpool, S. 2002. "The development of total quality management in Thai manufacturing SMEs: A case study approach", in *The International Journal of Quality and Reliability Management* (Bradford), Vol. 19, No. 4, pp. 380–395.

Tolentino, A. 1997. *Training and development of entrepreneur–managers of small enterprises* (Geneva, ILO).

United States Food and Drug Administration (USFDA). 2001. *Hazard analysis and critical control point principles and application guidelines*, available at http://www.cfsan.fda.gov/~lrd/haccp.html

—. 2005. National Advisory Committee on Microbiological Criteria for Food, Food and Drugs Administration, available at http://www.fsis.usda.gov/Science/

Wilkinson, A. 1999. "Employment relations in SMEs", in *Employee Relations*, Vol. 21, No. 3, pp. 206–217.

Wood, S. 1996. "High commitment management and payment systems", in *Journal of Management Studies*, Vol. 33, No. 1, pp. 53–78.

World Trade Organization (WTO). 2003. *World Trade 2003, Prospects for 2004* (Geneva).

—. 2004. Press release 373, 5 April.

—. 2005. *World Trade Report. Recent medium-term trends* (Geneva).

Wray, D. 1996. "Paternalism and its discontents: A case study" in *Work, Employment and Society*, Vol. 10, No. 4, pp. 705–715.

Yin, R. 1994. *Case study research: Design and methods* (Beverly Hills, CA, Sage) 2nd ed.